Books for Spiritual Growth

The 13 Blessings of Gratitude

Discover the Amazing Power of Biblical Gratitude

Book & Devotional Journal

Cynthia K. Johnson

Copyright © 2025 by Cynthia K. Johnson. All Rights Reserved.

All rights reserved. No part of this book may be reproduced in any form or by any electronic or mechanical means, including information storage and retrieval systems, without permission in writing from the author. The only exception is by a reviewer, who may quote brief excerpts in a review.

Unless otherwise noted, all Scripture is taken from the New American Standard Bible®, Copyright © 1960, 1962, 1963, 1968, 1971, 1972, 1973, 1975, 1977, 1995 by The Lockman Foundation. Used by permission. All rights reserved.

Scripture quotations marked NIV are taken from the Holy Bible, New International Version®, NIV®. Copyright © 1973, 1978, 1984, 2011 by Biblica, Inc. ™ Used by permission of Zondervan. All rights reserved worldwide.

Scripture quotations marked TPT are from The Passion Translation®. Copyright © 2017, 2018, 2020 by Passion & Fire Ministries, Inc. Used by permission. All rights reserved. ThePassionTranslation.com

Scripture quotations marked NKJV are taken from the New King James Version®. Copyright © 1982 by Thomas Nelson. Used by permission. All rights reserved.

Scripture quotations marked MSG are taken from *The Message*, copyright © 1993, 2002, 2018 by Eugene H. Peterson. Used by permission of NavPress. All rights reserved. Represented by Tyndale House Publishers.

Cynthia K. Johnson, Deeper Walk Ministries, Inc.
www.drcynthiajohnson.com
Printed in the United States of America
ISBN: 979-8-9927253-0-8

Stay in the know with upcoming books by signing up for my email list. I send out a new inspirational devotional teaching email once a month. Sign up at drcynthiajohnson.com

---

Contents

The Blessings of Gratitude 1
   Introduction 3
   What is Gratitude? 5
   The Origins of Ingratitude 7
   The 13 Blessings of Gratitude 31
      1. Gratitude Blesses Us With Divine Light to See 31
      2. Gratitude Blesses Us to Think Like Christ 36
      3. Gratitude Blesses Us With Abundant Grace 41
      4. Gratitude Blesses Us With Growing Faith 49
      5. Gratitude Blesses Us With Success 54
      6. Gratitude Blesses Our Purpose & Destiny 60
      7. Gratitude Blesses Us with Sustaining Strength 69
      8. Gratitude Blesses Us with Peace & Contentment 73
      9. Gratitude Blesses Us With God's Presence 79
      10. Gratitude Blesses Our Relationships 82
      11. Gratitude Blesses Our Physical & Emotional Health 88
      12. Gratitude Blesses us with a Powerful Weapon 94
      13. Gratitude Blesses Us With Generosity 100
30 Days of Gratitude Guided Journaling Exercises 105
Appendix 137
   How to Hear God Through Journaling 138
   Practical Ideas For Cultivating Gratitude Daily 146
   About the Author 149

The Blessings of Gratitude

Introduction

ON A VACANT LOT next to our home, a giant sign on a barrier across the crumbling driveway warns, "Danger: Do Not Enter." Towering overgrown live oak branches bend downward to guard the entrance. Wild vines and weeds obscure the path and give the area an eerie, unwelcome appearance.

The lot stands in the middle of a circle road that goes back to a county highway. Many people wander down this way, but when they see the warning sign, instead of continuing, they turn around and go back the way they came.

In a similar way, many of us have constructed "Do Not Enter" signs that hinder our Lord's blessings from coming into our lives.

God has given His children access to incredible treasures in the kingdom of God, yet many of us are not fully living in the abundant gifts and provisions He has promised.

We have constructed barriers around our hearts and lives that prevent us from fully experiencing His amazing peace, love, joy, and abundance. There are attitudes and beliefs guarding our lives that signal "Do Not Enter" to people around us and to our Lord.

These barriers can manifest in various ways, some of which include chronic discontent, dissatisfaction, disappointment, bitterness, pessimism, tendencies toward self-reliance, self-pity, and judgment.

Sometimes, these attitudes are subtle—like vines growing unnoticed until they choke out the abundant life we desperately desire. Other times, these attitudes can be bold and obvious noxious weeds, like negativity, anger, or rebellion.

These attitudes become spiritual roadblocks, hindering the abundant life God desires for us. They cause His blessings to bypass us and land in the lives of other believers who have grateful hearts!

The surprising truth we will explore in the following pages is that these feelings, attitudes, and habits can spring from the unseemly seed of ungratefulness. An ungrateful heart can prevent us from fully stepping into the peace, love, joy, abundance, and purposeful destiny God has prepared for us.

Yet, gratitude has the power to tear down these barricades and transform our lives in ways we never thought possible. The question is, will we choose to take down the barriers and enter the fullness of His abundance? Or will we allow the "Do Not Enter" signs to persist and keep us from the life He intended?

In Part 1, I will dive deep into the Biblical origins of ingratitude for a couple of sections. Then, based on this foundation, I will continue to share revelation about the 13 blessings of gratitude and their power to transform our lives spiritually, emotionally, and even physically. Plus, I will share a strategy that I have found to be a most helpful way to process the "Do Not Enter" feelings, attitudes, and mindsets we have all collected through the years.

Then, as a bonus, in Part 2, I have included 30 days of devotional verses with inspiration and journaling prompts to help you practice integrating Biblical gratitude into your daily life. Those "Do Not Enter" signs in our lives will have to come down!

What is Gratitude?

*"**Every good thing given and every perfect gift is from above**, coming down from the Father of lights, with whom there is no variation or shifting shadow" (James 1:17).*

THE OXFORD DICTIONARY says gratitude is "the quality of being thankful; readiness to show appreciation for and to return kindness." That's a helpful definition, but let's take it deeper by exploring how gratitude can shape our lives as children of our Creator Father in the kingdom of God.

God is the ultimate source of every good thing in our lives. And gratitude truly is more than a polite "Thank you." It is our heartfelt response to God's unwavering goodness and unfailing kindness.

It's a posture of humility and trust, recognizing that every blessing comes from Him. Gratitude can shift our focus from what we lack to the abundance of what we've been given and the miraculous possibilities that surround us.

Living with gratitude aligns our hearts with God's purposes. It fosters peace and strengthens our faith. It teaches us to be content even in difficult circumstances. Gratitude opens doors to joy, healing, and spiritual growth. It invites miracles and empowers us to live a victorious, purposeful life.

When we cultivate gratitude, we practice acknowledging God's blessings, yes. But we also step into a deeper relationship with Him and learn to trust that He is always working for our good in whatever life throws at us.

In this book, we will learn how to cultivate gratitude while becoming more aware of what God wants to reveal to us about gratitude and our lives. This isn't just about cognitive learning; it's about life transformation.

At the end of each section, you'll find reflection questions designed to help you engage with God personally. These questions are meant for you to ask yourself and ask our Teacher, Jesus. If this is new to you, don't worry. I've included a step-by-step guide in the Appendix to help you learn how to hear from God in this way.

All you need to do is ask the questions and write down your responses. As you follow along, God Himself will guide you, helping you to become more aware of your heart and His gentle voice in your life.

May God bless your journey of cultivating gratitude! He's already walking with you!

The Origins of Ingratitude

*"But **you said in your heart**,*
'I will ascend to heaven;
I will raise my throne above the stars of God,
And I will sit on the mount of assembly,
In the recesses of the north.
I will ascend above the heights of the clouds;
I will make myself like the Most High'" (Exek 14:13-14).

The Anointed Cherub

IN THE VERY BEGINNING before time as we know it, Satan lived on the holy mountain of God, surrounded by all the splendor and glory of Heaven. The Bible describes him as the "anointed cherub who guards."[1] The early church fathers referred to him as Lucifer, which means "shining one" or "light bringer" and also, "morning star," which describes him before his great fall. The Bible indicates that he occupied an exalted position in the heavens.

Lucifer most likely played a leadership role in Heaven's worship, as Scripture speaks of his being "crafted for music" with "pipes and timbrels" built into his very being.[2] His presence resounded with splendor, radiated light, beauty, and wisdom. He was uniquely created to reflect this glory back to the One who created him.

Yet, despite his high calling and unmatched glory among the creations, Lucifer's heart turned inward. Rather than pouring out gratitude and worship on his Creator, he craved glory for himself. He said, "I will ascend above the heights of the clouds; I will make myself like the Most High" (Exek 14:14).

---

[1] Ezekiel 28:14.
[2] Ezekiel 28:13 NKJV.

He got caught up in his own beauty, talent, and wisdom. He looked at God's glory and power with envy and jealousy. He thought he was better than others and could ascend to the heights of heaven to be the judge of all. He did not guard his own heart.

Lucifer became discontent with his place in God's kingdom. He refused his purpose and call and was dissatisfied with the way God made him. He let restlessness, discontent, resentfulness, bitterness, and pride consume him.

In this toxic state, Lucifer lured a third of the angels to follow his jealous, rebellious scheme to grab power and attempt to ascend higher than his own Creator. As a result of their sinful mutiny, God cast them down from the holy mountain and away from His presence.[3]

I don't know about you, but I have wondered how such pride could have taken root in a being created so perfectly and dwelling in such majesty. How could someone with everything—beauty, wisdom, honor, exalted position, and closeness to God—find a reason to crave more? Was all that he had simply not enough?

We know that God withholds nothing truly good for His creation. He is generous and gives us everything necessary for our well-being and fulfillment.[4]

What if discontent, greed, resentment, envy, jealousy, rebellion, offense, and pride could have first sprouted from a lack of gratitude? What if from the seed of ingratitude grew all Lucifer's sins?

Could it be that ingratitude took root and blinded him to the gifts he'd been given as a created heavenly being and led him down the path of dissatisfaction, pride, and rebellion?

---

[3] Isaiah 14:12.
[4] 2 Peter 1:3.

While Scripture does not explicitly state this, a thoughtful reflection on the Word suggests it as a possibility worth considering.

The Consequences

If this is so, then unfortunately, the infectious nature of ingratitude tragically contaminated a third of the other angels as well. The root of ingratitude seduced even the most glorious and blessed created beings on the mountain of God. It turned them away from their Creator Father's love, His blessings, and their divine purpose.

Even today, jealous, resentful, and prideful people often attempt to pull others into rebellion against what is right. Could this behavior stem from a heart of ingratitude? What might have happened if they chose to express gratitude for the blessings God had already provided?

If Lucifer had approached his Creator Father with a heart of gratitude, expressed his desires, and sought clarity, he would have found a loving response and true satisfaction.

But instead, he chose pride and self-will. He refused to humble himself, so he grew unsatisfied, jealous, prideful, complaining, resentful, and bitter. All his attitudes said, "Do Not Enter" to his Lord God, Creator of the Universe. And the results were devastating.

Through Lucifer's example, we are reminded how important it is to cultivate a grateful heart. As a creation of our Creator Father, gratitude keeps us aligned with our Creator's love and divine purpose for our lives. It helps us to see the abundance of His blessings and protects us from pride and dissatisfaction. A thankful heart turns our gaze back to God, the Source of our life and all good things.

Cultivating Gratitude

1. Think about when you felt envious of someone else's achievements or possessions. What were the underlying feelings driving this attitude? Jesus, what would you say to me about my perspective in this situation?[5]

2. Can you identify a time when you have allowed discontent or comparison to cloud your gratitude? How can you shift your focus to the blessings God has already provided?

3. Have you ever noticed how attitudes of discontent or resentment influence those around you? Can you think of a situation where your ingratitude affected others negatively? Jesus, what would you say to me about this?

_____
_____
_____
_____
_____
_____
_____
_____

---

[5] See the Appendix section, "How to Hear God Through Journaling."

The Ingratitude of Adam and Eve

*"**God blessed them**; and God said to them, "Be fruitful and multiply, and fill the earth, and subdue it; and rule over the fish of the sea and over the birds of the sky and over every living thing that moves on the earth." Then God said, "Behold, I have given you every plant yielding seed that is on the surface of all the earth, and every tree which has fruit yielding seed; it shall be food for you" (Gen 1:28-29).*

"The Lord God commanded the man, saying, **"From any tree of the garden you may eat freely; but from the tree of the knowledge of good and evil you shall not eat,** *for in the day that you eat from it you will surely die" (Gen 2:16-17).*

THE SEED OF INGRATITUDE didn't end with Lucifer's fall. When he was cast down from Heaven, he spread the same seeds in the Garden of Eden.

Adam and Eve were crafted in the very image of God, immersed in His love, and entrusted with the privilege of being His representatives on Earth. They lived in the beauty of Eden surrounded by abundance, and God gave them authority and dominion over creation. Above all, they enjoyed an intimate relationship with God Himself. They truly had everything they could want, and yet somehow, it wasn't enough.

The One Thing They Couldn't Have

God had given Adam a single command to not eat from the Tree of Knowledge of Good and Evil or they would die.[6] One day as Eve strolled past the forbidden tree, Satan entered the crafty serpent and seized the opportunity to plant a seed of doubt in Eve's heart. He lured her closer to its shiny fruit. His tactic was simple but

---

[6] Genesis 2:15.

powerful: He directed her gaze toward the one thing she could not have.

The serpent suggested God was withholding something essential from them, something that would make them wise. The temptation was never just about the fruit itself; it was about a lie that distorted God's character and made Eve believe she was missing out on something crucial.

In Genesis 3:1, Satan twists God's command, slyly asking, "Indeed, has God said, 'You shall not eat from any tree of the garden'?" In today's language, his question might sound more like, "Wait, really? God actually said you could not eat from ALL the trees?"

Manipulation and Discernment

Of course, this wasn't a genuine question. It was a manipulative tactic to suggest that God's command was unreasonable. Satan attacked God's authority and hinted that God was withholding something good. He suggested God was being unreasonable for placing a limitation on His human creation. Satan's words implied that God was spiteful, mean, selfish, and controlling—all qualities that belong to Satan himself, not to God.

In our fallen world today, scientists estimate there are nearly 100,000 species of trees. So, for Adam and Eve in a fresh, newly created world, obedience was about one tree. Satan twisted this one boundary to appear like a great injustice.

His underlying motive aimed to sow offense, ingratitude, and rebellion in their hearts. By magnifying what they couldn't have, he planted the idea that they deserved more and that God was holding back from them.

Satan questioned God's command and insinuated that Adam and Eve should feel shocked, hurt, and offended. Satan's underlying motives were to provoke an attitude of ingratitude and to suggest rebellion was smart and clever.

In tempting Eve, he subtly turned her attention to what she lacked rather than the abundance God had already provided. In doing so, he magnified the same ingratitude that led to his rebellion.

Satan's Timeless Tactic

Even today Satan's tactic hasn't changed. Many of us have listened to the same whisper in our hearts that diverts our attention from obedience and gratitude for God's abundant provision toward the one shiny thing we do not have. Our gratitude falters when the enemy tempts us to fixate on what we don't have, rather than all we've been given. However, cultivating gratitude is a powerful defense against the enemy's lies.

Adam and Eve were seduced away from pure devotion by the lusts in their heart. Like Lucifer before them, they allowed a seed of ingratitude to blind them. Instead of bringing their questions and desires to their Creator Father, they let ingratitude, dissatisfaction, and discontent guide their actions.

Imagine with me for a moment. What if, instead of listening to the serpent, Adam and Eve had taken their doubts and desires directly to God? What would have happened? I believe they would have found answers in His wisdom, fulfillment in His love, and reassurance in His care.

But rather than seeking the truth from their loving Creator Father, they chose to trust the subtle lie that they needed something more outside of God's care. That choice led to what theologians call the Great Fall. It loosed death in every form on the earth and separation from their Creator Father who loved them deeply.

Gratitude is a Safeguard Against Satan's Lies

Their history shows us this powerful truth that gratitude can be a safeguard against the enemy's seeds of doubt and unthankfulness. Gratitude redirects our hearts to our Source and reminds us that every good thing comes from Him.

When we embrace a lifestyle of thankfulness, we protect ourselves from deceptions that lead to pride, entitlement, rebellion, and separation from the One who loves us beyond measure.

Cultivating Gratitude

1. Ponder the struggle with ingratitude for Lucifer and Adam and Eve. How do their actions encourage you to guard your heart against discontent and cultivate gratitude? Jesus, what would you say to me today about this?
2. When you face unmet desires and unanswered questions, do you turn to God or try to fulfill these on your own? Do you turn to God in honesty and gratitude, or rely on your own understanding and self-sufficiency?
3. In what ways might you unknowingly cultivate ingratitude in your own life? Take a moment to ask Jesus about areas where dissatisfaction or comparison (or any of the other warning signs) may have taken root, clouding your view of God's plans and provisions.

_____
_____
_____
_____
_____
_____
_____
_____
_____

Jesus' Example of Gratitude

"Who, as He already existed in the form of God, did not consider equality with God something to be grasped, but **emptied Himself** *by taking the form of a bond-servant and being born in the likeness of men, being found in appearance as a man,* **He humbled Himself** *by becoming obedient to the point of death, even death on a cross." (Philippians 2:6-7).*

IN STARK CONTRAST to Lucifer and Adam and Eve, Jesus had no seed of ingratitude in His heart, though He faced countless opportunities for such a seed to take root. As the son of God, Jesus knew that all power and authority belonged to Him.[7] Yet, His human response was never one of pride or entitlement. Rather, as our verse above states, He "emptied Himself." He surrendered His heavenly privileges and position, choosing to take on the lowly form of humanity. He became a servant—a "nobody" by worldly standards—to fulfill His purpose.

Where others fell into sin by grasping for power, position, and things that weren't theirs, Jesus took the opposite path. Instead of striving for power, prestige, or earthly gain, He surrendered His divine privilege. He knew who He was, and all He had in the kingdom, yet He didn't cling to that status.

Instead, He willingly laid it down to serve and save humanity. He embraced humility, lived with a heart full of gratitude, and demonstrated complete trust in His Father's will.

Some Biblical Examples of Jesus Living in Gratitude

During His time on earth, Jesus modeled humility and surrender to His Father's will in both miraculous moments and difficult

---

[7] Matthew 28:18.

moments. For example, before the miracle of feeding the five thousand men plus women and children, Scripture records that Jesus after "having given thanks, He distributed . . . as much as they wanted" (John 6:11). There was a miraculous multiplication of five loaves and two fish from a little boy's lunch into enough to feed a multitude, with twelve baskets left over!

Similarly, in another event, He gave thanks and trusted His Father to provide abundantly for over four thousand people.

Jesus also showed unwavering gratitude in moments of grief. At the tomb of His friend, Lazarus, He lifted up His eyes and declared, "Father, I thank You that You have heard Me" (John 11:41). Even in this moment of profound grief, He expressed gratitude and recognized His Father's faithfulness to hear and answer prayer for miracles.

During the Last Supper, knowing He was facing torment and death, we see a profound moment of gratitude. Scripture says, "And when He had taken some bread and given thanks, He broke it and gave it to them, saying, 'This is My body, which is being given for you'" (Luke 22:19). Jesus expressed his thanks and willingly gave Himself for a world filled with unthankful people. His gratitude was not contingent on other people's responses but rooted in His unwavering love and obedience to His Father.

These are just a few examples recorded in Scripture, but they reveal a life deeply rooted in unwavering trust and extraordinary gratitude.

Jesus' Gratitude Demonstrated Surrender and Obedience

For Jesus, a heart of thankfulness was the foundation of humility and obedience. In John 6:38 Jesus said, "For I have come down from heaven, not to do My own will, but the will of Him who sent

Me." His submission to His Father's plan reflects a heart of gratitude, not rebellion.

You see, ingratitude breeds selfishness and rebellion, as we saw with Lucifer. Ingratitude breeds dissatisfaction and all sorts of lust and self-sins. Yet, Jesus' life demonstrates the opposite. He trusted His Father's perfect will even when confronted with misunderstanding, persecution, suffering, and death on the cross.

People disappointed Him, turned on Him, and betrayed Him. One of His closest disciples sold Him out. Faithful friends denied knowing Him. His own family didn't understand or believe in Him. When He needed them most, they all left Him. Yet, through all of this, Jesus remained faithful in surrendering to and obeying God's will, proclaiming, "Not My will, but Yours be done" (Luke 22:42).

Jesus didn't rally people to His side in rebellion. He didn't feel that His Father was holding out on Him. He didn't throw a pity party, and say, "Woe is me. I have it so bad." He didn't throw a tantrum and fuss about why other people have it better. He didn't grow stubborn, bitter, angry, jealous, or resentful.

Instead, He humbled Himself, even unto death. "For the joy set before Him, He endured the cross" (Heb 12:2). His attitude echoes Psalm 40:8, which says, "I delight to do Your will, my God; Your law is within my heart." Even in the face of unimaginable suffering, Jesus chose to fulfill His purpose.

Jesus endured the worst adversity of His life by remaining silent before His accusers.[8] Instead of arguing or retaliating, He prayed, "Father, forgive them; they do not know what they are doing" (Luke 23:34).

Though the cross was excruciating, He chose not to be offended, jealous, bitter, or resentful. He trusted God's plan. He

---

[8] Mark 14:61; Isaiah 53:7.

had peace in knowing His suffering had a purpose far greater than the present pain.

Through Jesus' example, we see that gratitude is not dependent on circumstances. It is a choice. It is a decision to recognize and rely on God's faithfulness no matter what we face.

Jesus' life shows us a radically different way of living, one that contrasts sharply with the world's self-focused approach. When our hearts are surrendered to God's will, gratitude flows naturally and enables us to trust Him fully.

In prayer and His presence, we find the strength to rely on His goodness and perfect timing. Like Jesus, when we live in gratitude, surrender, and obedience, we discover the true peace, love, joy, and fulfillment that only God can give.

Cultivating Gratitude Like Jesus

1. Jesus "emptied himself." As a disciple of Jesus, what does it mean for you to "empty yourself"? Jesus, what do you say to me about this?
2. How do you respond when life doesn't go as planned? Do you find it easy or challenging to surrender your will to God's? In what ways can you cultivate gratitude, even when you don't understand God's plan?
3. What does it mean to you that gratitude is not dependent on circumstances but is a deliberate choice? How can you choose gratitude today, even in difficult or uncertain situations?

_____
_____
_____
_____
_____
_____
_____
_____
_____
_____
_____
_____
_____

We Joyously Give Thanks

*We are **joyously giving thanks** to the Father, who has qualified us to share in the inheritance of the saints in Light. For **He rescued us** from the domain of darkness and transferred us to the kingdom of His beloved Son, in whom **we have redemption, the forgiveness of sins**" (Col 1:12-14).*

IMAGINE RECEIVING a large inheritance from a distant relative whom you scarcely knew. Initially, you may not grasp the full significance of this gift, but as you gain a deeper understanding of what it encompasses, you come to appreciate its true value, and it fills your heart with profound joy and gratitude.

This is the way it is when we are first born again. We may not fully understand what our new inheritance means, but we are initially full of joy and gratitude, much like the woman with the alabaster jar of expensive perfume in the book of Luke.

In a powerful moment, a woman, known to be a sinner, most likely a prostitute, anoints Jesus' feet with an alabaster jar of expensive perfume.[9] Though others were present at this dinner, she was the one who most valued His presence. She came to Jesus with a heart full of gratitude and wept so much that her tears washed His feet. She dried them with her hair and anointed them with perfume. Scripture says she continually kissed His feet from the moment He entered.

She extravagantly honored Him because she loved Him dearly and appreciated the depth of His forgiveness. Jesus responded to those who criticized her, saying, "She was forgiven many, many sins, and so she is very, very grateful. If the forgiveness is minimal, the gratitude is minimal" (Luke 7:47 MSG).

---

[9] Luke 7:36-50.

Similarly, we, too, have received the ultimate gift of Jesus' forgiveness. By paying the price for my sins and yours, He made it possible for us to live in a relationship with Him, free from the chains of guilt and condemnation. Through Jesus' life, death, and resurrection, he gave us the ultimate gift—the gift of forgiveness, eternal life, and reconciliation to our covenant with our Lord in His kingdom.

This is the most profound gift we could ever receive!

And yet, how often do we forget to express our gratitude for this gift? The example of the woman with the alabaster box was written so that we could understand the nature of our Lord as we passionately pour out our thanks for this gift. He longs for us to extravagantly offer our hearts in thanksgiving, in powerful moments, and also as a lifestyle.

At the end of this passage, Jesus says to the woman, "Your faith has saved you, go in peace."[10] As you may already know, the original Greek word for "saved" most times is the word *sozo*, which means salvation from sins, but also the healing of our spirit, soul, and body!

This woman came to Jesus with thanksgiving and faith and received wholeness! Just as this woman's passionate gratitude and faith brought her wholeness and peace, so too can our thankfulness draw us closer to our heavenly Father, where we find love, mercy, help, and wholeness in every area of our lives![11] It's an inheritance gift we don't have to wait to receive—it's already ours, and it's something we can joyously give thanks for every single day.

---

[10] Luke 7:50.
[11] Hebrews 4:16.

Cultivating Gratitude & Joy

1. Like the woman with the alabaster jar, how can you express your gratitude to Jesus for His forgiveness and grace? What specific acts of thankfulness can you offer today?
2. Reflect on Colossians 1:12-14. How does this passage encourage you to live joyously in gratitude? Jesus, what does this mean for me?
3. How can you cultivate a heart that values the gift of Jesus' forgiveness more profoundly?
4. Are there areas in your life where you have difficulty accepting God's forgiveness? What might be keeping you from fully embracing the peace and freedom His forgiveness offers? Jesus, show me more about this.

_____
_____
_____
_____
_____
_____
_____
_____
_____
_____

Gratitude Is A Choice

What is the source of quarrels and conflicts among you? Is the source not your pleasures that wage war in your body's parts? You lust and do not have, so you commit murder. And you are envious and cannot obtain, so you fight and quarrel. **You do not have because you do not ask.** *You ask and do not receive, because you ask with the wrong motives, so that you may spend what you request on your pleasures (James 4:1-3).*

UNFORTUNATELY, WE ARE NOT automatically born with a thankful attitude. We must learn to be thankful through practice and experience. Toddlers do not say, "Thanks mom for giving my sister cookies before me." We must teach toddlers to say "please" and "thank you." Our fallen human nature tends toward envy and strife, pushing and shoving to get our own way.

In our fallen human nature, we can be like toddlers. We complain, push, and shove to get our own way. Then we blame others. Additionally, our toddler nature makes us feel bad and makes everyone around us feel bad as well. A negative, complaining spirit grieves our own soul and everyone around us. Yet, everyone loves a person who is thankful, joyful, and kind.

As adults, we must remember to be nice, kind, and thankful, and it becomes easier if we have already established a lifestyle habit of gratitude. Learning to practice giving thanks in all circumstances is a discipline that trains our minds toward positivity and goodness rather than negativity.

Even research shows that developing a lifestyle of thankfulness changes the chemistry in our brains and we feel happier. Thankfulness is a skill we can learn that will change our attitudes and create a happier life! We must make an effort to practice gratitude daily because even good habits can easily slip away.

Gratitude is a Lens We See Through

Gratitude is a choice. It is a daily decision to see life through the lens of God's provision rather than through the lens of lack. In a world where we are constantly bombarded with messages of glittery things we should have, we can easily fall into the habit of focusing on what we don't have. The world teaches us to measure success by material wealth, career achievements, or social media following. But God invites us to look beyond the superficial and recognize the richness of His grace, mercy, and love in our everyday lives.

God wants us to choose His ways above the ways of the world, and His way of thinking above the world's way of thinking. He wants us to remember His provision and miracles when we encounter day-to-day life.

For example, the Israelites faced a choice after God had miraculously delivered them from slavery in Egypt. As the days went on, they got weary in the scorching desert and forgot God's miracles and provision. They forgot the brutal task masters in Egypt and their deliverance from the Ten Plagues. They forgot how God had parted the Red Sea as all the people walked safely across on dry ground, and then how He drowned their enemies in the collapsing waters. They forgot the provision of water from the rock. They grumbled, complained, and blamed.[12]

They complained against Moses, against Aaron, and even against the Lord God! They focused on what they lacked and missed the fact that God was providing for their every need.

How often do we do the same?

It's easy to overlook God's daily gifts, especially when life feels uncertain or difficult. But when we choose to be thankful in all

---

[12] Exodus 16:2-3.

circumstances, we align our hearts with God's truth that He is always enough!

We Learn To Recognize God is Working

Gratitude isn't about denying hardship or pretending everything is magical. It's about recognizing that even during challenges, God is working all things together for our good.[13] When we make a conscious choice to be thankful, we begin to see the fingerprints of God in both the big moments and the small ones. Every breath we take, every meal we eat, every pet we enjoy, every flower we observe, every friendship we relish—these are all reflections of God's faithfulness.

Choosing gratitude transforms how we experience life. Instead of seeing obstacles, we begin to see opportunities for God to reveal His glory. When we shift our focus from what we lack to what God has already given us, peace floods our hearts.

The Apostle Paul, who faced imprisonment, shipwrecks, countless trials, and constant death threats, understood this truth well. He wrote to the Philippians, "I have learned to be content in whatever circumstances I am" (Phil 4:11). This means he had plenty of opportunities to choose whether to be content or discontent. His contentment wasn't based on his circumstances, but on his choice to trust in God's plan.

How Do We Grow in Gratitude?

We all face moments of ingratitude. Even Eve, who lived in the perfection of Eden, allowed discontent to take root in her heart. Instead of rejoicing in God's abundant provision, she fixated on what she didn't have. That ingratitude opened the door to the enemy's deception. The serpent lured her with false promises,

---

[13] Romans 8:28.

tempting her to believe she was missing something vital—when, in truth, she already had everything she needed. She was made in God's image, walked in His presence, and lived in His provision. She just needed to remember to be thankful! So, how do we cultivate this habit of gratitude?

1. **Decide To Look For The Good**

First, gratitude begins with an intentional decision to look for God's blessings each day until it becomes a habit. At first, this may feel like an act of discipline, but as we continue, the Holy Spirit softens our hearts and shifts our perspectives. Over time, gratitude becomes more than a practice—it becomes a way of life.

2. **Talk To God About Everything**

Secondly, we must bring all our questions, frustrations, and desires to our Creator. James reminds us, "You do not have because you do not ask" (James 4:2). Sometimes, our lack of gratitude stems from not asking God for understanding or help. Other times, we fail to see the divine potential in what we already have.

Instead of dwelling in worry, fear, offense, or dissatisfaction, we can turn to God with open hearts. When we live in constant conversation with our Heavenly Father, it transforms how we see life. Scripture says that Moses understood God's ways while the people only witnessed His acts. We can grow in wisdom, understanding, and trust as we ask Him questions and listen for His answers.

Gratitude flourishes when we recognize His voice, discern His guidance, and see His hand at work in every situation. When we choose gratitude, it keeps us aligned with His will and purposes.

3. **Get To The Roots**

All this is hindered, however, when we have negative stuff in our hearts. Have you seen an x-ray of a tooth? It has roots that go down deep. Unthankfulness can be like an infection that travels down into the roots of a tooth. The dentist must cleanse and disinfect the canals within the tooth's roots so that the tooth can be saved. When God deals with our unthankful hearts, it can be like a root canal.

However, I pray we will allow the Holy Spirit to search out and cleanse the deep roots of unthankfulness we may not even know exist before they become infected and painful!

The enemy sows seeds of ingratitude all through our lives, and sometimes they hide deep in the crevices of our soul, in places we do not notice. When we decide to invite God to do His work, He will not leave infection in our roots. Expect Him to call your attention to things you did not know were in your heart.

4. Intentionally Cultivate a Lifestyle of Gratitude

On a hopeful note, if we intentionally cultivate a lifestyle of thankfulness, it automatically takes care of many of the selfish sin seeds in our souls before they become infected!

And hooray for you—you've chosen to grow in this amazing fruit of gratitude! Gratitude can destroy all the "Danger: Do Not Enter" signs that hinder God's blessings of peace, love, joy, and abundance from flowing into our lives.

In the next section, we'll explore 13 incredible blessings of gratitude and how they propel us forward in spiritual growth. Consider the reflection questions for this section, then we will dive into the blessings of gratitude.

Cultivating Gratitude to Grow

1. What "glittery things" in the world pull your focus away from God's provision? Jesus, what is distracting me from recognizing Your faithfulness?
2. Do you bring your frustrations and questions to God, or do you hold on to them? Jesus, what would you say to me about this?
3. Jesus, am I striving for anything outside of Your will? Am I fixating on something I should not?
4. When facing difficulties, how do you typically respond? How can you intentionally choose gratitude and look for God's hand at work even in challenging circumstances?
5. Are you willing to allow the Holy Spirit to cleanse those deeper areas to heal and restore your heart? Jesus, what "roots of unthankfulness" might be hidden in my heart?

_____
_____
_____
_____
_____
_____
_____
_____

Enjoying The 13 Blessings of Gratitude?

If this book has blessed you, would you take a moment to leave a review on Amazon? Your review helps spread the message of gratitude, faith, and spiritual growth—impacting more lives with the Good News of Jesus. Thank you for being a part of this journey!

The 13 Blessings of Gratitude

1. Gratitude Blesses Us With Divine Light to See

"I am the Light of the world; he who follows **Me will not walk in the darkness, but will have the Light of life**.*" (John 8:12)*

OFTEN PEOPLE SAY when they are saved, "I saw the light." And in a very real way, this is true; Jesus shined His light into our hearts and revealed our need for Him. In that moment, we recognized our brokenness, our sin, and our need for salvation. By His grace, we were transferred from the kingdom of darkness into the kingdom of light. We became a new spirit creation in Christ. Our human spirit was reborn instantly.

However, our minds, wills, and emotions are still saturated with the stain of Adam and Eve's sin. We walk in the Light, but hidden corners of our fleshly hearts remain smudged with darkness and require the radiance of Christ. We can invite His light into the hidden corners of our hearts, where it exposes the dust but also the beautiful, amazing possibilities and unexpected blessings.

Gratitude Expands Christ's Light in Our Hearts

When God declared, "Let there be light," light erupted across creation and filled every void. In the same way, the Light of Christ opens the eyes of our hearts and brings divine insight that dispels darkness in our lives.[14]

When I first began my gratitude journey, I was a negative and judgmental person. I was miserable and stuck in many areas of my life and did not know how to get unstuck! I did not realize how bad

---

[14] Ephesians 1:17-18.

I was, but I desperately wanted to grow in my relationship with God. When we invite Him to work in our lives, He does not leave us in our messes! He shines His light into our lives to bring revelation, understanding, and power!

I was doing a lot of scrapbooking with my teenage girls, so the Lord directed me to take a picture and/or document something I was grateful for each day for a year. Yes, an entire year! That process began a transformation in me and my thinking.

I would like to say my transformation was instant, or that a single year of practicing gratitude fixed me. Sometimes deep-rooted attitudes take more time, but God did give me a strategy. He gave me a concrete idea of what I could do on my part that would help change my life from the inside out.

I can say that I have extravagantly experienced all these blessings of gratitude that I will talk about in the next sections. And yet the life of gratitude continues to arrest my selfish thoughts and push me towards the love of God. It continues to bring light to my circumstances because I do not always have the mind of Christ!

Sometimes we all struggle to see as God sees. Our vision becomes clouded by worry, doubt, fear, and the limitations of our earthly perspective. The Apostle Paul prays we would see and know with God's enlightenment the riches, glory, and surpassing greatness of God's power toward us!

> *"I pray that the* **eyes of you heart may be enlightened** *so that you will know what is the hope of His calling, what are the* **riches of the glory of His inheritance in the saints**, *and*

*what is the **surpassing greatness of His power toward us** who believe" (Eph 1:18:19).*

Seeing God's Potential In The Ordinary

God's great power is with us, in us, and all around us! Yet, our problem is seeing it! Consider the moment God called Moses to deliver His people from slavery in Egypt. Moses felt inadequate and uncertain. But God asked him a simple question, "What is that in your hand?" (Exodus 4:2). Moses held an ordinary shepherd's staff, but God used that staff to split the Red Sea, bring plagues on Egypt, and demonstrate miracles. Moses' everyday, ordinary staff became a tool for God's miraculous works.

The message here is profound. Moses didn't realize the potential of what he already held in his hand until God opened his eyes to see its potential.

While our experiences with God may not be quite as dramatic as Moses' burning bush experience, we have amazing potential in our hands as well! We do not always recognize the potential of what God has already placed in our hands. Even a simple talent, a small opportunity, or a common relationship can serve as a supernatural catalyst for God's miraculous work when we see it through His eyes.

The Power of Gratitude to Open Our Eyes

Some things can either **open** our eyes to God's miraculous possibilities or blind our eyes. Prayer, Scripture, a genuine desire to know the Lord, and yes, gratitude, all open our eyes to what God wants to use to bless us!

On the other hand, fear, complaints, jealousy, doubt, and disappointment act like a thick fog over our spiritual sight. They block our ability to see God's abundant provision.

Gratitude has the power to shatter the fog and shift our focus from what we think we lack to what the Lord already placed before us. A thankful-hearted person trusts that God can use the small or ordinary and multiply its potential for His glory.

The enemy wants us to believe that we are lacking, that God is holding out on us. But when we cultivate a heart of gratitude, we stand in defiance of that lie. We recognize that everything we have is a gift from God. And if we are in relationship with Him, He provides exactly what we need when we need it.

Jesus Opens Our Eyes

After Jesus' resurrection, two of His disciples walked and talked with Him along the road to Emmaus without recognizing Him. Their grief and confusion blinded them to Jesus' presence. It was only when Jesus broke bread with them at the meal, that Scripture says, "their eyes were opened, and they recognized Him" (Luke 24:30-31).

The verse doesn't specifically say He gave thanks in this instance, but even as we saw earlier, when Jesus broke bread He gave thanks.[15] I find this fascinating! As He gave thanks in prayer, their eyes were opened. As He gave thanks and broke the bread, the bread multiplied for the five thousand. Also, as He gave thanks to His Father for hearing His prayer, Lazarus came to life again.

There is amazing power in giving thanks! And not just for those in Bible days! It is for us here and now! Giving thanks opens our eyes to see Jesus! And He blesses us with divine light to see! When we give thanks, He opens our sight to His amazing and miraculous provision! He opens our spiritual eyes to see more grace and goodness in all our circumstances—and the miracles might be already in our hands!

---

[15] A couple references are Matthew 15:36; Matthew 26:27.

Cultivating the Blessing of Gratitude for Spiritual Sight

1. Jesus, I pray that you would enlighten the eyes of my heart as Eph 1:18 says. What would you speak to me about this?
2. What "ordinary" things in your life might God be inviting you to view with new eyes? Like Moses' staff, reflect on how simple, everyday aspects of your life could become channels of God's power and purpose when approached with gratitude. Jesus, what are you shining your Light on in my life today?
3. Are there areas of your life where you struggle to see God's goodness? Consider how giving thanks could shift your heart to be receptive to God's possibilities.

2. Gratitude Blesses Us to Think Like Christ

*"And do not be conformed to this world, but **be transformed by the renewing of your mind**, so that you may prove what the will of God is, that which is good and acceptable and perfect" (Rom 12:2).*

HAVE YOU EVER FOUND yourself stuck in a cycle of negative thinking—quick to judge, quick to complain, or quick to assume the worst? We all do at times. But what if there was a simple, yet powerful, way to break free from those thoughts and step into a mindset of grace, peace, and faith?

Gratitude is that key.

Gratitude does more than just shift our perspective; it actively transforms our thought patterns. Our minds are incredibly powerful, and the thoughts we allow to dwell in our minds shape our lives. Scripture urges us, "Do not be conformed to this world, but be transformed by the renewing of your mind" (Rom 12:2).

When we train our minds in gratitude, we are not just being optimistic—we are aligning our thoughts with God's thoughts. We can transform our lives by renewing our minds, as our focus verse for this section above teaches.

Our thoughts can be influenced by the world, our flesh, the devil, or God Himself. I have found that learning to practice gratitude, is one of the simplest and most powerful ways we can transform our minds from the world's way of thinking to God's way of thinking.[16]

---

[16] Along with consuming large amounts of the Bible and ongoing conversations with God.

When we intentionally focus on gratitude, we begin to train our minds to think as God thinks—thoughts filled with redemption, grace, hope, possibility, and unconditional love.

Scripture tells us that we have the mind of Christ through the Spirit of Christ within us. Yet this gift must be activated and cultivated. God gives us the choice, and our natural ways often resist. We find ourselves torn between negative, judgmental thinking and God's higher, more gracious thoughts.[17]

Practicing Gratitude Transforms Our Thoughts

For example, I once attended a seminar at a church where my thoughts immediately turned critical. "This presentation is disjointed, confusing, and unorganized," I thought. I began to judge the presenter as being a poor teacher. Right then, I had a choice. I could continue in criticism, or I could pause and invite Jesus into my thoughts.

So, in my mind, I asked, "Jesus, what do you think about this?" I heard this in my heart, "You should be grateful he is willing and obedient to address these issues." I quickly shifted into gratitude! I became grateful for the presenter's willing heart, and also the grace God was extending to me in that moment! With a changed heart, I was able to receive the lesson with openness and humility. What started as a frustrating experience turned into a life-changing seminar.

When we make the choice to align our thinking with God's, even in moments of judgment or frustration, we invite His peace and grace into our hearts. That's the power of gratitude.

---

[17] 1 Corinthians 2:6-16.

Training Our Minds to Think Like Christ

If we want to think with the mind of Christ, we must stay vigilant about our thoughts. With a practice of daily gratitude, our thought patterns can begin to mirror His thoughts—thoughts anchored in peace, love, grace, discernment, and endless possibilities. This doesn't mean that negative thoughts won't come; they will. But with gratitude as our guide, we can recognize them for what they are—distractions—and choose to replace them with thoughts of thankfulness and hope.

In moments when we feel overwhelmed by negativity, we can pause and ask, "Jesus, how do You see this?" His perspective is always higher, wiser, and more gracious than our own. And when we choose to think as He thinks, our entire outlook on life shifts.

Transforming Our View of Challenges

As another example, I remember when some relatives were visiting. They complained nonstop about how our tiny town was being overwhelmed by rapid growth. Subdivisions were popping up everywhere with thousands of new households each month moving into town, not to mention the traffic congestion.

Their negativity was draining, and after they left, I felt unsettled. I asked the Lord for His light on the issue, and He said to me, "A vibrant and growing community is a blessing."

God's view transformed my view! His thoughts transformed my thoughts. Growth, while challenging, is a blessing. Instead of joining in the negativity, I could embrace gratitude for the new life and potential in our town. Of course, growth of any kind produces change and struggles but is a blessing nonetheless!

It is important to turn our thinking from negative and fearful complaining toward thankfulness, positivity, and faith by establishing what God thinks in a matter. This is how gratitude transforms our thoughts: it takes our limited, fearful perspective and opens our eyes to the possibilities that God sees.

Personally, I learned a lot of prideful and negative thought patterns growing up. So, it has been super helpful for me to learn how to turn to my Teacher and ask what He thinks of a thing. Then I can be more discerning in my thoughts.

The Life-Changing Power of Gratitude

Constant complaining and pessimism drain our energy and hinder our ability to experience genuine joy and gratitude. Even when we don't understand, we can trust God to turn situations for our good. And as we practice the habit of being thankful, gratitude soon becomes the lens through which we view life. We begin to see opportunities where others see obstacles. Then our lives begin to reflect God's goodness, and we experience His hope, peace, love, and joy. Not only are our minds transformed, but our lives are transformed as well! Gratitude truly blesses us and teaches us to think like Christ!

Cultivating Gratitude for the Mind of Christ

1. When you reflect on your current thought patterns, do you find they are more often negative or hopeful? Jesus, what would you say to me about this?
2. Decide and declare that you have the mind of Christ, and you will actively practice thinking the thoughts of God, starting with gratitude. Ask the Lord to wash your mind from worldly thought patterns.
3. Recall a recent time when you felt caught in negativity. How might pausing to ask for God's perspective have transformed that moment? Is there anything you could ask Him right now about that moment?

_____
_____
_____
_____
_____
_____
_____
_____
_____
_____
_____
_____

3. Gratitude Blesses Us With Abundant Grace

*"And God is able to **make all grace abound to you** so that always **having all sufficiency in everything**, you may have an abundance for every good deed" (2 Cor 9:8).*

IMAGINE STANDING BENEATH a powerful waterfall, the water pouring over you endlessly. No matter how much you try to catch in your hands, there is always more. The water is abundant, unceasing, and refreshing. This is God's grace: an ever-flowing, never-depleting, all-sufficient outpouring in our lives. He doesn't give just enough; He gives in abundance, overflowing into every area of our lives.

And just as His grace flows endlessly, our response to it matters. One of the simplest yet most powerful ways we acknowledge His abundant grace is through gratitude.

Interestingly, grace and gratitude are deeply connected, both in Scripture and in our everyday experiences. We often say "grace" before a meal, but have you ever considered how deeply grace and gratitude are intertwined? Our habit of saying grace points to a spiritual truth that giving thanks releases a fuller experience of God's loving kindness and goodness toward us.

The Definition of Grace

Many times, we hear grace defined as God's unmerited divine favor, and this is true. We do not deserve God's mercy, goodness, or favor. Yet, He grants us amazing mercy, unconditional goodness, graciousness, kindness, and favor![18] God's love toward us is immeasurable and always abounding!

---

[18] Summarized from Luter, A. Boyd. "Grace." In *The Lexham Bible Dictionary*, edited by John D. Barry, David Bomar, Derek R. Brown, Rachel Klippenstein,

The Apostle Paul used the word grace as a divine help and empowering favor. Grace is God's overflowing goodness and help and that works on our behalf to equip us to live in victory and fullness in every area of our lives!

The Passion Translation expands our understanding of this truth when it says, "Yes, God is more than ready to overwhelm you with every form of grace, so that you will have more than enough of everything —every moment and in every way. He will make you overflow with abundance in every good thing you do" (2 Cor 9:8).

Prayer and Thanksgiving Release Grace

God's empowering grace is released into our lives by prayer and thanksgiving. Philippians 4:6 tells us, "In everything, by prayer and petition, with thanksgiving, present your requests to God." Prayer with thanksgiving is a posture of faith that opens the door for God's abundant provision and power.

Jesus Himself modeled this truth. Before performing miracles, He prayed and gave thanks. When He fed the five thousand, He took the loaves, gave thanks, and then distributed them, leading to an abundance that fed the multitude.[19] Prayer with thanksgiving preceded the manifestation of abundant grace.

A Humble Heart Positions Us For More

We can actively position ourselves to receive more of God's abundant grace. As James 4:6 (TPT) declares, "God resists the proud but **continually pours out grace to the humble**." Gratitude and pride cannot coexist. A thankful heart is a humble heart. When we see through the eyes of gratitude it humbles us and expands our capacity to receive more of God's empowering grace.

Douglas Mangum, Carrie Sinclair Wolcott, Lazarus Wentz, Elliot Ritzema, and Wendy Widder. Bellingham, WA: Lexham Press, 2016.
[19] John 6:11.

Consider two different people I observed at church on Sunday. One person seemed distracted throughout the service—constantly going in and out during worship, whispering to her neighbor, and sending text messages all during the sermon. Week after week, she has been present but not fully engaged.

The Holy Spirit works in such delicate and intricate ways that we sometimes miss His what He is doing when we allow distractions to pull away our focus. Just as Eve overlooked the glory of Eden and was drawn away by what she thought she lacked, we, too, can become so familiar with God's blessings that we take them for granted. We get caught up in our own desires and forget to be thankful.

However, I also saw someone who approached the service with a completely different attitude. This person was deeply grateful just to be there and expectant for what God was going to do. She worshiped wholeheartedly, listened attentively to the sermon, and eagerly took notes. She was fully engaged and ready to receive. Her gratitude created a posture of humility, and in that humility, she positioned herself for more of God's presence and grace.

When we approach God with thanksgiving and humility, we create space for His abundant grace to flow freely into our lives. A heart postured in gratitude is a heart that remains open to His leading, sensitive to His voice, and receptive to His blessings.

Humility and gratitude don't just position us to receive—they magnify God's glory in our lives. They shift our focus from ourselves to Him, from our distractions to His presence, and from lack to abundance. They bless us to receive the abundance of God's grace that empowers us to walk in His abundant blessings.

The Mindset Shift from Lack to Abundant Grace

Sometimes we can have trouble seeing the abundance of God's blessings. As our key verse reminds us though, "God is able to make all grace abound toward you (bless you), so that always having all sufficiency in everything, you may have an abundance for every good deed" (2 Cor. 9:8). His grace is not limited or scarce—it is overflowing, always available, and more than enough.

Yet, too often, we live spiritually nearsighted, unable to see beyond our immediate circumstances. If this is the case, we might have a scarcity or poverty mindset.

A scarcity mindset keeps us focused on what we lack rather than on the limitless grace of God. It traps us in a cycle of fear and anxiety about the future, clouding our ability to recognize the blessings already in our lives.

When we allow a poverty mindset to take root, it distorts our vision—like wearing blinders that block our view of God's abundant provision. Instead of seeing opportunities, we see obstacles. Instead of trusting in God's sufficiency, we dwell on our insufficiencies. But gratitude has the power to break this cycle.

By shifting our focus from what we lack to what we have—and ultimately, to the One who provides—we open our hearts to the flow of God's empowering grace.

I grew up with a poverty mindset, so without realizing it, my default response to my daughter's requests was always "no" until God began to show me that He was not saying "no."

It wasn't always about the money; it was about my mindset. I had to pause and ask, "Is this a true financial limitation, or is it fear speaking?" God was teaching me to shift from fear to faith, from lack to abundance, and it started with gratitude. He was inviting me to let go of my limited perspective and embrace the limitless possibilities of His provision.

Sometimes we hold tightly to this idea of scarcity or lack. While I was writing this, I had a brief vision of a hand clenched so tightly that the muscles strained, and the knuckles turned white. This is a clear picture of how we often grip our fears, worries, and doubts about not having enough.

But God invites us to do the opposite! Instead of clinging to fear, He invites us to open our hands and release to Him this idea of lack, our worries, and our need to control, which is really fear in disguise.

He asks us to trust Him with what we have and what we don't have. He asks us to give our concerns to Him with thanksgiving and then watch in expectation. When we release our grip on fear and scarcity, we make room to receive something far greater: His amazing, abundant grace.

Gratitude Transforms Our Perspective

Shifting from a mindset of lack to one of abundance **begins** with giving thanks! When we choose gratitude, we reposition our hearts to trust in God's grace rather than be consumed by what we feel is missing. Thanksgiving opens our eyes to the blessings already present in our lives and makes room for even greater provision.

God's grace is always at work, but when we allow lack and fear to cloud our perspective, we fail to see it. It's like standing in a dark room, unaware of the beauty around us—until someone flips the switch. Gratitude is that switch. It illuminates God's faithfulness, revealing the abundance that was there all along.

Consider the Israelites in the wilderness. Each morning, they gathered manna, the daily provision straight from God's hand. They were learning a vital truth that grace is given for today. They didn't need to hoard it or fear for tomorrow because God's provision was new each morning.[20]

This same principle applies to us. One of the most powerful spiritual laws I have learned is that God's grace is available fresh each day. Just as His mercies are new every morning (Lamentations 3:22-23), so is His grace. We can ask for grace for the day, and He will supply it in abundance.

When family members or friends call me burdened by struggles, I often ask, "Have you asked for your grace for the day?" Time and again, I've seen how this simple prayer transforms our days, which in turn generates much thanksgiving!

Blessings of Abounding, Multiplying Grace

Jesus declared, "I came that they may have life, and have it abundantly" (John 10:10). This is not a life of barely getting by but one overflowing with His grace, provision, and goodness. When we embrace an abundance mindset rooted in gratitude, we begin to see God's hand in every aspect of our lives. We recognize Him as Jehovah Jireh, our faithful Provider, who supplies not just enough—but more than enough.

Living with a heart of thanksgiving positions us for greater faith and unlocks the spiritual principle of multiplication. Just as Jesus took the young boy's five loaves and two fish and multiplied them to feed thousands, He can take whatever we offer—no matter how small—and expand it beyond what we could imagine. But multiplication begins with surrender. When we open our clenched fists of fear and trust Him with what we have, we make space for His abundant grace to flow.

Imagine waking up each morning with your hands open, expectant, and ready to receive the fresh grace God is pouring out

---

[20] Exodus 16.

for the day. His provision is never stale or depleted! It is always new, powerful, and always sufficient. Today, ask for His grace, give thanks for His provision, and step into the truth of His Word: "God is able to make all grace abound to you so that always having all sufficiency in everything, you may have an abundance for every good deed" (2 Cor 9:8).

An open hand not only receives His abundant blessings, but it also releases them to others. As we freely receive, we freely give, becoming vessels of His multiplying grace in the world.

Cultivating the Blessing of Gratitude for Grace

1. Consider how prayer with gratitude and humility is like the key to a wellspring of blessings. What practical steps could you take to embrace a posture of thanksgiving and humility before God?
2. Jesus, what amazing things would flow from my life if I embraced your empowering grace more fully each day? Ask for grace for the day.
3. Are there areas in your life where a scarcity mindset might be holding you back? Are there areas you struggle to trust God's abundance? Which fears can you let go of? How would living with an open hand change your life? Jesus, what would you say to me about this?
4. Jesus said He came to give life abundantly (John 10:10). Do you believe you are living in abundance? In the area where we lack, we can rely on grace more. Jesus, what would you speak to me about this?

4. Gratitude Blesses Us With Growing Faith

*"Therefore, as you have received Christ Jesus the Lord, so walk in Him, having been **firmly rooted and now being built up** in Him and **established in your faith**, just as you were instructed, and **overflowing with gratitude**." (Col 2:6-7).*

IN NORTHERN FLORIDA, sabal palm trees have become a familiar part of newer landscape designs. Most of these palms are harvested from swampy areas, plucked up without a root ball, and transported to nurseries. They arrive stripped of their fronds, looking lifeless. It is common to see piles of sabal palm trunks tossed into a pile with no water or soil. I am amazed they survive at all. When they are finally planted, they must be firmly secured with wooden stakes to keep them upright until they gradually develop new roots and become established.

Being Planted in Gratitude Establishes Us

The Apostle Paul's words above illustrate a similar process in our spiritual lives. Being "rooted" in Christ "and overflowing with gratitude" is essential to establishing our faith. Gratitude is an essential nutrient in fertile soil that nourishes our roots of faith. It helps our roots to grow deeper and more resilient.

Like the sabal palm, our spiritual life may seem dormant at times. Yet, when we are planted with gratitude, we grow roots that build a strong structure that establishes us in our faith in God!

It is said that an established palm tree can withstand hurricane-force winds because its roots grow deep and its trunk is flexible, allowing it to bend without breaking. Likewise, when our faith is deeply rooted in gratitude, we become resilient and flexible in the face of life's storms. Challenges may come, strong winds of adversity may blow, but a heart established in thanksgiving remains steadfast.

Being Established in Gratitude Grows Our Faith

Just as deep roots establish and strengthen a tree, gratitude establishes and strengthens our faith. This connection between gratitude and faith is beautifully illustrated in the Biblical example of the ten lepers.

As Jesus entered a village one day, ten lepers, isolated from society, stood at a distance and called out for healing. "They raised their voices, 'Jesus, Master, have mercy on us!'"[21]

When Jesus heard them, He responded, "Go and show yourselves to the priests." In obedience, they turned to go and as they walked, they realized all ten were healed. But only one, a Samaritan man, returned to Jesus to give thanks.

This act of giving thanks became more than just good manners for this man, who was not even a Jew, it was an expression of faith. His thanksgiving opened the door to an even greater miracle. Jesus said to the man, "Your faith has made you whole."

This is a great example of how faith and gratitude are interconnected. The man returned to give thanks and Jesus said, "Your faith has made you whole." This man's leprous, scarred, and possibly deformed or crippled body was more than healed; it was made new. The other nine lepers were healed, but this man was made whole! Because of his gratitude, he received complete wholeness in his body, mind, emotions, soul, and spirit.

Giving thanks opens the gates for healing and miracles of wholeness in our lives. Just like this leper, we also with a humble heart of gratitude will receive more than healing; we will receive wholeness from Jesus' faithfulness—if not immediately then

---

[21] Luke 17:11-19.

definitely eventually! Keep asking, believing, and trusting with a heart of gratitude! And even if your faith for healing of things like leprosy is not strong yet, don't give up because we are being rooted and established! And we are growing in faith!

Thankfulness Grows Our Faith In God's Provision

Gratitude keeps us anchored in God's promises, reminding us that no matter the storm, He is our faithful refuge and strength! When we choose thankfulness, it opens our hearts to expect and trust that God will provide for us not only today but in all the days to come.

For instance, when we are truly thankful that God provided groceries today, it gives us confidence to trust Him to provide again tomorrow. If we are grateful for the job He gave us today, we believe He can and will provide another job if we need one tomorrow. When we appreciate the opportunities God has granted us today, we naturally grow in faith that He will open new doors in the future.

Every act of gratitude builds upon the last, strengthening our faith and creating a firm foundation of trust. Each experience of God's faithfulness, acknowledged with gratitude strengthens and extends our roots sending it deeper into the earth to make us unshakable even in life's storms.

This is the kind of faith that becomes deeply rooted and continuously grows. It establishes us in trust and expectancy, preparing our hearts for God to move in greater ways—just as He did for the grateful leper who received complete wholeness.

Remembering God's Faithfulness Builds Faith

David provides another example of this principle. When he faced Goliath, he recalled how God had given him victory over the lion and the bear.[22] Because he had seen God's hand before, his faith was strong enough to confront the giant.

Gratitude is both a response to what God has done and an expectation of what He will do. Why would He entrust us with more if we are not grateful for what He has already given? Why would He open new opportunities if we're too busy complaining about our current situation?

When we thank God today, we're acknowledging His goodness and faithfulness. We reinforce our trust that if He provided for us today, He will be there for us tomorrow as well. As gratitude overflows, so does our faith, enabling us to stand strong—like deeply rooted sabal palms—through every season of life, even the fiercest storms.

---

[22] 1 Samuel 17:34-37.

Cultivating the Blessing of Gratitude for Faith

1. Like the sabal palm, have you ever experienced a time when you felt uprooted or stripped down? How did gratitude help you establish new spiritual roots? How has gratitude helped you remain steadfast in difficult seasons?
2. Think about the example of the ten lepers. Jesus, what do you want to show me about the connection between giving thanks and wholeness?
3. What past experiences of God's provision inspire you to trust Him more fully now? What current blessings can you thank God for to help build a foundation of faith for tomorrow?
4. What are some areas of your life where you need to cultivate a deeper sense of gratitude? How can you be intentional about expressing thankfulness daily?

_____
_____
_____
_____
_____
_____
_____
_____
_____

5. Gratitude Blesses Us With Success

For I know the thoughts that I think toward you, says the Lord, thoughts of peace and not of evil, **to give you a future and a hope** *(Jeremiah 29:11).*

YOU'VE LIKELY HEARD the phrase "success brings success." While this may hold some truth, I'd like to suggest that in God's kingdom, gratitude blesses us with success. Throughout the Bible gratitude and success go hand in hand. So in this section, we will continue to examine how gratitude opens our hearts to the fulfillment of God's promises and His success!

Consider the example of the children of Israel wandering in the wilderness.[23] They had experienced God's miraculous provision over and again, first in the miraculous protection from the plagues in Egypt, deliverance from Egypt, and crossing the Red Sea. The miracles continued as God turned bitter waters sweet and sent miraculous provisions of manna and quail every morning. They saw the astonishing power of God on Mount Sinai and His remarkable presence in the Tabernacle. God supernaturally guided them with a pillar of cloud by day and a pillar of fire by night. He abundantly and powerfully provided for their every need, so that even their shoes didn't wear out. They had every reason to be thankful, yet they grumbled and complained continuously.

They could have entered their promised land a number of times before they did because geographically it's less than a couple of weeks' journey from Egypt. But at each critical junction, they were

---

[23] Exodus.

not thankful. They grumbled, complained, and rebelled at God's ways.

In the third year of their journey, God offered them a new opportunity to enter the Promised Land. Moses sent twelve spies to scout out the abundant land of Canaan, symbolically called a land flowing with milk and honey.[24]

When the spies returned, they brought back reports of a land rich and plentiful. The grapes were so large that two men carried a single pole between them with one hanging cluster of grapes.

However, the land also contained the sons of Anak—the giant. Ten of the spies looked at the people and the fortified cities and shrank back in fear. They saw themselves as grasshoppers in comparison to the people of this land. They saw the amazing qualities and possibilities of the land God promised to give them, but they were not able to believe they could possess these promises.

However, Caleb and Joshua held to the vision of God's promise. They saw beyond the giants to the abundance. They believed God would do what He said and give them the land. Where the other ten spies saw obstacles, Caleb and Joshua saw opportunities.

The Children of Israel, who were already steeped in a mindset of ingratitude, could not embrace Joshua and Caleb's positive report. They had fallen into a pattern of ingratitude and doubted God at every turn. They already had a long history of grumbling, complaining, negativity, and fear, and were faced, yet again, with another test of attitude, and they failed.

Their attitude angered the Lord God, in so much as God swore they would not enter His rest or receive His promises.[25] God waited until the unbelieving generation had passed away before allowing their children to enter the land of promise.

---

[24] Numbers 13.
[25] Hebrews 3:11.

The only exceptions were Joshua and Caleb! They valiantly and boldly entered the success of their promises. They conquered the territory they were given and lived to see peace and prosperity!

Their example illustrates a clear warning for us today: a complaining and ungrateful attitude blinds us to God's provision. It opens the door to fear, lack, insecurity, scarcity, and anxiety. It leads to rebellion, failure, and missed opportunities. Ingratitude keeps us from God's best and provokes Him to anger.

Yet, gratitude opens the door to God's favor, faith, success, and living in God's amazing promises of success and abundance.

Gratitude Brings Success In Our Lives Today

An attitude of gratitude opens the door to a life of true success. We can see this truth not only in the Bible but also in our everyday lives.

In my work with people struggling with addictions and life-controlling issues, I observed that gratitude often serves as a predictor of success. Those who approached recovery with genuine thankfulness for the help they received were far more likely to overcome their struggles.

In contrast, those who lacked gratitude often dropped out of rehabilitation and returned to destructive behaviors. This pattern illustrates the profound impact gratitude can have in bringing success in all areas of our lives.

Comparison Blinds and Robs Us

Just as the Children of Israel compared themselves to the successful people of Caanan, we can sometimes compare ourselves to others, especially in the age of social media.

I was discussing this with a friend, Lori, who found herself trapped in this cycle of comparison.[26] Every time she opened social media, she saw vacations, new homes, and perfectly posed family photos. She felt like her life wasn't measuring up.

One day, instead of continuing to scroll, she stopped and thanked God for her morning coffee and the laughter of her kids. That small shift sparked a chain reaction of gratitude. Lori realized her life was already rich in many ways social media couldn't capture.

Social media was causing all kinds of icky feelings in her heart. But, when she paused to focus on gratitude, she felt herself break free from the trap of comparison. She was able to refocus her heart on the things that mattered the most.

We tend to scroll through curated snapshots of other people's lives and silently measure our lives against theirs. We can feel like grasshoppers. But this constant comparison robs us of peace, joy, and faith. It blinds us to our blessings and all of God's amazing possibilities.

Instead of looking outward to measure our worth, we can pause to look upward to God, the giver of every good gift. We can cultivate a habit of gratitude, which brings light to see the blessings we already have and strengthens our faith for even greater blessings!

Gratitude Blesses Us With Success

Just as Joshua and Caleb saw their Promised Land through eyes of faith and gratitude, we too can unlock doors of opportunity and blessing when we live with thankful hearts.

God rewards gratitude and faith! We see it in the example of the leper who returned to thank Jesus, in the lives of Joshua and Caleb, and we can see it in our lives as well.

---

[26] Not her real name.

Gratitude doesn't only recognize God's blessings—it also invites them. It positions us to receive the fullness of His promises and empowers us to walk in victory. When we choose gratitude, we choose God's best for us, and we step into the success He's already prepared for us to walk in!

Cultivating the Blessing of Gratitude for Success

1. How does the story of Joshua and Caleb encourage you to view your future with faith and thankfulness? Reflect on how their example of gratitude and trust in God's promise can inspire you to approach your own goals with thankfulness and faith. Jesus, speak to me about this.
2. Are there areas in my life where complaints, dissatisfaction, or negative thinking are blocking my success? Jesus, what do you say to me today about this?
3. Think of an obstacle in your life right now. Ask Jesus how you can view this from His perspective. Jesus, what can you show me about this?
4. Before logging into social media, write down three things you're thankful for today. Reflect on how this changes your perspective.

6. Gratitude Blesses Our Purpose & Destiny

"It is God's will that you should be sanctified" (1 Thess 4:3-5).
"For those whom He foreknew, He also predestined to become conformed to the image of His Son" (Rom 8:29).
"In everything give thanks; for this is God's will for you" (1 Thess 5:18).

WE OFTEN WAKE UP to our phone's buzzing alarm and fumble for its off button. Groggy, we get up and begin to face our daily routine. Sometimes, we wonder, "Is there more? Am I really in God's will?" Life feels ordinary, yet our hearts long for something more. Many of us pray, "Lord, what is my purpose," and we sit back and wait for a miraculous sign.

In our Bibles, we are told that we were created as His children, shaped by our Creator Father's love for a relationship and destined to reflect His glory. We were created for a divine purpose! Our single most important purpose is to love our Creator Father with all our hearts and to enjoy His love as His beloved child![27]

Created By Love And For Love

We were created by Love and for love. Jesus teaches us the greatest commandment is to love the Lord our God with all our heart, soul, mind, and strength! This is our foundation. From this love relationship flows everything else in our lives, including other calls and assignments He has for us.

When we focus on our primary purpose as a love relationship with God, we grow strong in our identity as His royal sons and daughters. It is in this relationship that we find the confidence to

---

[27] Matthew 22:37-40. I explore purpose and identity extensively in *Return to Eden, Book 1*.

embrace our uniqueness and the courage to step into further calls and assignments He has prepared for us.

Gratitude Strengthens Our Purpose

During times of struggle or questioning, I often remind myself of this truth: I am a child of God. My primary purpose is to love Him and receive His love. This simple realization has the power to comfort, strengthen, encourage, and renew our perspective.

Many of us were raised in a world that operates on performance. In school, we earn grades for our work. In life, we gain favor by doing things well. But with God, we do not have to earn anything. His love is freely given, His grace an unwavering gift. We do not have to strive to deserve His love.

I have stood still in moments of overwhelming questions and whispered, "All I have to do is love the Lord and receive His love." In those moments, it was enough, and I was grateful!

Thankfulness Brings Fulfilment

When we embrace our primary purpose to love God, we remember His unchanging love for us. Thanksgiving shifts our focus from uncertainty to assurance, from striving to trust in His love and grace.

Thankfulness swells into praise and leads us into His presence (Which we will explore further later!). In His presence, we find peace, strength, fulfillment, and the assurance that He is with us and working for us, regardless of our momentary circumstances. We rest in the knowledge that He is always with us, working in and through us, shaping our destiny with His love.

Friends, you are called, chosen, and deeply loved. If you are loving on Jesus, you are fulfilling your primary purpose! Your secondary purpose and other assignments are unfolding even now, and your destiny is secure in His hands.

Sanctification: A Key to Fulfilling God's Purpose for Our Lives

For Christmas one year, I remember buying my daughter a modeling dough toy. It came with little molds shaped like a boy, a girl, a dog, and a cat. She would press the dough into the mold, open it, and see the image of a girl, boy, dog, or cat. Yet, each time, excess dough squished out along the seams, which she had to carefully trim with a plastic knife.

In our Christian journey, we are much like that modeling dough image. As we grow in gratitude and conform our minds and hearts to Christ's image, God lovingly shapes us and trims away what does not reflect Him. Though it may feel uncomfortable at times, it is a necessary part of our transformation. It is His will for all His beloved children as He prepares us for our next assignment or call in His kingdom.

As we continue to grow in our relationship with our Lord, we desire to live a life pleasing to Him. The section verse above reminds us, "It is God's will that you should be sanctified." Sanctification means being set apart as holy and purified for God's purposes. It is both a momentary event—when we are born again and our spirit is made holy—and a lifelong process of transformation into the image of Christ.

Because none of us are perfect or all-knowing, God lovingly works to shape our earthly clay throughout our lives. This process of sanctification continues as He refines our thoughts, attitudes, and actions to reflect more of His character.

Giving Thanks in All Things

It is essential to learn how to give thanks in every circumstance, even when the process feels difficult. Sometimes, sanctification feels like being pressed into a mold or having excess parts of ourselves cut away. Yet, even in these moments, we can look to

Jesus, who gave thanks on His way to the cross. When His life seemed to fall apart, He trusted His Father's goodness, believing that all things would work together for good.

As our focus verse reminds us, giving thanks in all things is God's will. When God moves us into new assignments, He often asks us to step outside of our comfort zones. Yet, when we cultivate a heart of gratitude, we can respond as David did when he said, "I delight to do Your will, O my God" (Psalm 40:8).

I often find myself repeating this verse when God stretches me in ways that feel uncomfortable. Gratitude shifts my perspective. It reminds me that even when I feel unsteady or unsure, God is working in my life and deepening my trust in Him.

Living Gratitude On Purpose

God uses our everyday lives to work out His sanctifying purposes in us. Many people feel stuck in jobs that seem mundane or uninspiring. However, when we approach our work with gratitude, we begin to see His divine purpose in every task.

I remember my father worked at a factory job for a number of years. Instead of viewing it as merely a way to earn a paycheck, he saw it as his mission field. During lunch breaks, he hosted a Bible study and prayer group. What could have been a monotonous routine became an opportunity to minister to others.

As Colossians 3:23 encourages us, "Whatever you do, do your work heartily, as for the Lord rather than for men." When we shift our focus from seeing work only as a duty to seeing it as a way to glorify God, it transforms us and others around us. My father's factory job became a platform for God's kingdom, simply because he chose to work with a thankful heart.

God can use anything we do, no matter how small or ordinary, to bless others and fulfill His purposes. Gratitude opens the door to see how He is moving in the most unexpected places. He continues to take us from glory to glory, from one assignment to the next! When we live with an open and thankful heart, we discover the success and purpose God has prepared for us.

Cultivating Gratitude for Purpose & Destiny

1. Have you ever considered your primary purpose to love God and enjoy His love? Lord, what would you speak to me about this?
2. In what ways can you express gratitude for your current work situation, even if it feels mundane or unfulfilling? How might viewing your work as a mission field or ministry change your attitude toward it?
3. What new assignments or calls do you sense God preparing you for? How can gratitude help you embrace these opportunities with faith and courage?
4. Consider an area of your life where God is shaping you. Write about what He is "trimming away" and thank Him for the transformation, even if it feels difficult.

Toxic Attitudes Hinder Our Divine Purpose

Just as gratitude blesses our purpose and destiny, the opposite is also true: ingratitude can create a barrier that prevents us from walking fully in our purpose and destiny. Other attitudes that tend to hang around with ingratitude are bitterness, unforgiveness, disappointment, stinginess, crankiness, a grumbling complaining spirit, etc.

When we allow negative emotions to take root, they can cloud our perspective, drain our joy, and keep us from experiencing the abundant life God intends for us. It's as if we are putting up a "Do Not Enter" sign to God.

These attitudes create barriers, much like those that caused the children of Israel to wander in the wilderness for 40 years. Instead of walking into their promised land, they remained stuck and held back by their negativity and unbelief.

These toxic mindsets block God's work in our lives and hinder His blessings. So, how do we let them go? Scripture gives us a powerful key: "Whatever you bind on earth will be bound in heaven, and whatever you loose on earth will be loosed in heaven" (Matt 18:18). Begin by declaring, "I loose bitterness, unforgiveness, and negativity from my soul." Or simply pray, "Jesus, I give You my pain, disappointment, and anger." Whatever comes to mind, release it to Him. Open your hands—physically if you need to—and give it all to Him.

He is more than capable of handling every hurt you've experienced. He is more than able to deal with those who have wounded you. We can trust Him to take care of us *and* them.

When we release toxic emotions, we unclog our hearts, making room for the goodness God longs to pour into our lives. But when our thoughts remain consumed by negativity, we are, in effect, telling God, "No Trespassing!" Gratitude, however, removes the barriers. A thankful heart stands wide open, ready to receive the abundance of blessings He desires to lavish upon us.

Your Heavenly Father wants you to thrive in life and relationships. His thoughts toward you are always good! As you cultivate gratitude, you align yourself with His will. And as you do, He will faithfully lead you into the fullness of your destiny.

A Prayer to Release Toxic Barriers

Pray this prayer: Lord Jesus, I ask you to forgive me for all the times I have missed the mark of your best. I loose all these feelings of _____ from my soul. I open my hands and turn loose of all these things. I give _____ to you. I forgive all the people who have hurt me. I leave them in your hands. I trust you to take care of me and them. I ask you to cover me in your blood and empower me by your Spirit to walk in a life of gratitude. Shine your light into my life and show me how to go forward starting with forgiveness and thankfulness. I choose to be thankful in all things. Thank you for your mercy and grace! What else would you say to me right now?

_____
_____
_____
_____
_____
_____
_____
_____
_____
_____

7. Gratitude Blesses Us with Sustaining Strength

"...Nor let us tempt Christ, as some of them also tempted, and were destroyed by serpents; **nor complain,** *as some of them also complained, and were destroyed by the destroyer. Now* ***all these things happened to them as examples, and they were written for our admonition"*** *(1 Corinthians 10:6-11 NKJV).*

WHEN YOU ARE NOT seeing success and when a hard season grows long, it can be tempting to give in to impatience and ingratitude. Some of the largest obstacles we face in these wilderness seasons are the thoughts that arise.

For example, we may experience impatience with our situation, we may question why it seems God isn't providing, or we long for what we think was better in the past. We might be hurt, offended, or disappointed. These kinds of thoughts can cloud our perspective, making our present season seem unbearable.

The children of Israel experienced this very struggle in Numbers 21. God delivered them from slavery and promised to take them to a land of their own. By the time we read Numbers 21, they had been in the wilderness for 40 years and 7 months.

You probably know the story of how they had faced obstacle after obstacle and had become impatient because of the length of the journey. So, their impatience caused them to grumble again. They did not understand their time was almost finished in the wilderness. It would only be six months until they would cross the Jordan into the long-awaited and promised Caanan land.

However, in their discontent, bitterness, and disappointment, they spoke against God and Moses, saying, "Why have you brought us up out of Egypt to die in the wilderness? For there is no food and no water, and we loathe this miserable food" (Num 21:4-5).

And this wasn't exactly true; they had food and water, just not the food or water they had in Egypt. And if they had not complained so incessantly, they would have been in a life of abundance sooner!

They forgot how God miraculously delivered the entire nation from slavery and provided faithfully all along their journey. They forgot their clothes never wore out. They forgot the presence of God with them. They complained about the manna, the quail, the water, and well, everything. They disrespected God's leaders, prophets, and God himself.

Instead of believing for the future, they began to look back 40 years ago at their days in slavery, thinking perhaps it wasn't so bad after all. Their complaints escalated into blaspheming God, rejecting His chosen leader, and despising the very blessings God had provided.

This deep ingratitude angered God and opened the door to severe consequences. God lifted His protection for a moment and allowed fiery serpents to invade the camp. Many people tragically died, and only when the people repented did God, in His mercy, send deliverance.

Their example serves as a powerful reminder for us. When we allow impatience and ingratitude to take root, we lose sight of God's goodness and the ways He sustains us, even in the hardest of times. The Israelites' complaining attitude caused them to forget the bondage they were rescued from and the promise that awaited them.

When we intentionally train our minds to be grateful, we shift our focus from what we lack to God's provision and promises. We begin to notice that even in difficult times, there are things to be thankful for, whether it's the strength to endure, the people who encourage us, or the lessons we learn. We can learn to recognize all the little things God provides along the way. We can ask to see His purpose for the circumstances we are in. He is faithful to give us understanding when we ask.

I have never had a time when I asked for encouragement—not in an ungrateful or demanding way, but a thankful-but-I'm-hurting kind of way, that God did not bring encouragement in some way. He will encourage you too, simply ask in faith.

As we practice being thankful in all things, we remember that God is always working for our good, even when the path ahead isn't clear or is getting long. Thankfulness reminds us that He has a plan, and He is with us through every difficulty. When we embrace thankfulness, we align ourselves with God's heart and God's thoughts. Thankfulness opens our eyes to see His provision, grace, and sustaining strength in our lives—even in a wilderness season.

Cultivating the Blessing of Gratitude in Hard Times

1. Are there areas in your life where you find yourself longing for the past or feeling that God isn't providing? Give those feelings to Him. Jesus, what would you say to me about this?
2. Think of a difficult situation in your life right now. What thoughts or emotions tend to arise? How can you shift these thoughts to focus on God's faithfulness?
3. God promises to encourage us when we ask. Ask for His encouragement and be open to hear or see what encouragement comes your way. If you do not hear immediately, expect to see something soon.

8. Gratitude Blesses Us with Peace & Contentment

"Be anxious for nothing, but in everything by prayer and supplication **with thanksgiving** *let your requests be made known to God. And the peace of God, which surpasses all comprehension, will guard your hearts and your minds in Christ Jesus." (Philippians 4:6-7).*

GOD'S PEACE—the kind that exceeds our understanding—comes to us when we bring everything to Him in prayer *with* thanksgiving. True peace is not the absence of trouble but the presence of God in the middle of it. Jesus said, "In the world you have tribulation, but take courage; I have overcome the world" (John 16:33).

When I first heard this verse, it did not make sense to me. I was irritated because I thought, "I have all this trouble, and am glad for you, Jesus, but what about me? How does that help me?" It seemed distant and irrelevant to my struggles.

In time, I began to understand that Jesus' words held a key. He was not promising a life without trouble but offering triumph through my relationship with Him. The path to peace required me to ask for His help in prayer and thanksgiving, and then trust Him while also standing firm against the schemes of the enemy. Through my ongoing conversations with Him, the One who overcame the world, I could experience His instructions that would bring victory, peace, and contentment into my life.

Breaking Free from Barriers of Unrealistic Expectations

While gratitude can help bring us peace and contentment, unrealistic expectations often stand as barriers that keep us from fully experiencing God's peace. To experience true peace and contentment in our souls, we must confront and release the pressures that rob us of peace.

One of the enemies' tactics is discontentment. Sometimes discontentment comes not from our circumstances so much as the unrealistic expectations we carry.

Some of us may live under this kind of unrealistic pressure in our daily lives. Perhaps we've been raised to strive to live a so-called "perfect" or "ideal life." Maybe social media or the culture around us pressures us with unrealistic expectations. These expectations can seep into our relationship with God, making us feel we must be "perfect" Christians to please Him.

But this pressure doesn't come from our Heavenly Father. He knows we are imperfect; that's why Jesus came. Jesus alone is perfect, and through Him, we are covered in His righteousness, with our flaws and all.

We can give these unrealistic expectations to Him! God simply wants our honesty; He will help us with all the rest! Like David, who poured out his heart to God honestly and openly, we, too are free to come to Him just as we are.[28]

God's love and acceptance are not based on our "perfect" performance but on His grace—His amazing grace! When we grab onto this amazing, unchanging, unconditional love and grace with gratitude, it frees us from the exhausting pursuit of performance and perfection.

The Apostle Paul shares with us what God told him, "But He said to me, 'My grace is sufficient for you, for my power is made perfect in weakness.' Therefore, I will boast all the more gladly about my weaknesses, so that Christ's power may rest on me" (2 Corinthians 12:9 NIV).

---

[28] Psalm 62:8.

We can let go of the pressure to be perfect and rest in God's amazing love and be thankful. We can give all our feelings and desires to Him in prayer and thanksgiving. And He will give us His perfect peace!

Gratitude Helps Us Choose Contentment

You may have heard life described as a hamster wheel, the kind where the hamster goes around and around on a plastic wheel, never going anywhere. Sometimes we get caught up in circumstances that make us feel like we are continually spinning in the wheel of life.

Our ancient enemy will try every trick he can to keep us stuck in life and our walk with God, even if it is with good and necessary things. He often tries to trip us with lies, whispering that relentless, excessive striving—a better job, a bigger house, greater status—will bring satisfaction. Yet, as Ecclesiastes 1:14 reminds us never-ending pursuits are like chasing the wind, always elusive and ultimately unfulfilling.

Like Eve in the Garden of Eden, we become vulnerable to these seducing lies when we focus on what we lack. The serpent's temptation magnified the one thing Eve didn't have, blinding her to the abundance God had already provided.[29]

Gratitude, however, will shift our perspective in any circumstance. When we pause to give thanks, it's as though the fog of distraction lifts. We see the blessings already before us, and the insatiable desire for "more" fades into the background.

Thankfulness makes way for peace and contentment. It reminds us that true fulfillment is not found in chasing the world's fleeting distractions but in cherishing the good gifts God has already given us.

---

[29] Genesis 3:1-6.

You Can Trust Your Heart's Desires to the Lord

"Delight yourself in the Lord; And He will give you the desires of your heart." (Psalms 37:4).

Desiring more is not necessarily wrong. God delights in blessing His children with good things, just as we want to shower our children with gifts, especially on Christmas.[30] Yet, rather than live in anxious and continual striving, He invites us to bring our desires to Him, seek His wisdom, and trust His perfect timing.

Instead of struggling in our own strength to grasp what we think we need, we can place our desires and dreams in His hands with gratitude. We can surrender all to Him and exchange our anxious struggle for peace that settles our souls. As Philippians 4:7 assures us, the peace of God will act as a guard for our hearts and minds when we trust Him with our requests and approach Him with thanksgiving. We can trust Him with our most fervent desires and dreams! For He may have placed them in our hearts to begin with.

The verse above says that when we delight in God, He will give us our desires. You see, when we delight in Him, He aligns our desires with His perfect will. We pursue His heart's desires, and He fulfills the desires of our hearts. As we trust Him with our desires our anxious striving is replaced with peace and contentment.

God's Promise to Turn Our Struggles Into Good

Life can be such a struggle sometimes. We struggle with our inner heart desires and also external life problems, many of which we do not have control over. Yet, through every kind of struggle, we can be grateful for the promise that God is with us. Even when answers to prayers seem far off, He will never leave us or forsake us. He has a way of working all things together to turn out for our

---

[30] Matthew 7:11.

good.[31] Even when the enemy intends harm, God can transform those situations into opportunities for our blessing. Just like He turned Joseph's brothers' betrayal into a way to save nations, He can redeem our hardships for His purposes.[32]

Living a life rooted in gratitude can change our perspective about these struggles. It brings light to see God's hand at work and fosters peace and contentment as we trust God's plan and timing.

When we choose gratitude, we step into a confidence that God is with us and for us. We can experience God's peace and contentment that defies our circumstances. As we hold on to thankfulness, we experience the fullness of God's peace, which guards our hearts and minds and draws us closer to His unfailing goodness.

---

[31] Romans 8:28.
[32] Genesis 50:20.

Cultivating the Blessing of Gratitude for Peace & Contentment

1. Are there areas of your life where you feel the pressure to be perfect? How does gratitude for God's grace and unconditional love free you from this burden? Jesus, speak to me about this.
2. Are there things you're tempted to focus on because they seem "better" than what you have? Jesus, what would you say to me about this?
3. When was the last time you brought your desires to God? Ask Him about these now and be aware of spontaneous thoughts that come to mind.
4. How can you practice contentment in your current circumstances, trusting that God knows what is best for you? Jesus, what do you think?

_____
_____
_____
_____
_____
_____
_____
_____
_____

9. Gratitude Blesses Us With God's Presence

"Enter his gates with thanksgiving and his courts with praise" (Psa 100:4; 150:1).

IN PREVIOUS SECTIONS, we have seen where thanksgiving was closely linked with revelation, grace, faith, success, purpose, strength, peace, and contentment. In this section's verse, we see that thanksgiving is linked with praise and entering the courts of God's presence.

The Tabernacle of the Old Testament was a physical type and shadow of how things work in God's kingdom. In the Tabernacle, anyone could enter through the gates into the courtyard. Yet only the priests could enter the Holy Place, then only once a year could the high priest, with fear and trepidation, enter into the Most Holy Place.

However, Jesus came and ripped the veil that separates all of us from the Most Holy Place of God's presence. As believers, we are all permitted to enter the most holy places in God's presence! And the first step is thanksgiving!

If we want more of God's presence in our daily lives, according to the above verse, we must go through the gate of thanksgiving and continue with praise into His courts.

Praise is a natural result that comes from a heart full of thanks. The more gratitude we develop in our hearts, the deeper we can connect with God in praise. Maybe you have experienced a time when you felt your inner heart swell with love and gratitude that resulted in a "hallelujah" or a "praise the Lord!"

One time I was practicing growing my faith in God's provision, and He told me to give my car to a single man who was raising two children. My husband agreed with me, and I gave my car away. Well, I was left without a car. I had been working on a car lot and had seen a minivan I loved. It was a Dodge minivan with a sliding door on the driver's side. I can't explain how "in love" I was with this van. It doesn't make sense. However, the Lord provided me with a green (my favorite color) Dodge minivan. I was so thankful. Every time I got in my minivan, I thanked the Lord! Then I would start thinking about the goodness of God and begin praising and worshiping Him, which then led to some wonderful times in His presence. Can you see the progression that begins with giving heartfelt thanks that results in praise, then worship?

> *"You are holy, O You who are enthroned upon [inhabit] the praises of Israel" (Psalm 22:3).*

Psalms 22:3 tells us that God takes up residence in the place where praise dwells. In other words, the Lord lives in the middle of praise. Heaven is a place of continual worship of God, both day and night.[33] So, when we learn to dwell in an attitude of continual thanksgiving, praise, and worship, we learn to dwell in the atmosphere of heaven here on earth.

If we are aware of it, even the slightest thanks or praise from our hearts will usher us into God's presence. This too is a skill you can learn and practice.[34] If we want to keep the doorway open for more of God's presence in our daily lives, we can cultivate a continual attitude of thanksgiving and praise.

Thanksgiving and praise are our pathway into God's presence. As we cultivate a daily lifestyle of gratitude, we make more and more room for our Lord in the residence of our hearts.

---

[33] Revelation 4:8.
[34] For more, see my book, *How to Practice the Presence of God*.

Cultivating Gratitude

1. Can you recall a time when heartfelt thanksgiving led you into a deeper moment of praise and worship? How did it impact your sense of God's presence?
2. What emotions or thoughts arise when you express gratitude? How does it shape your ability to worship?
3. Are there situations or mindsets that hinder your ability to give thanks? What "Do Not Enter" signs might you have unknowingly placed in your heart that could be keeping you from fully entering into God's presence?

_____
_____
_____
_____
_____
_____
_____
_____
_____
_____
_____
_____
_____
_____

10. Gratitude Blesses Our Relationships

"Let no unwholesome word proceed from your mouth, but only such a word as is good for edification according to the need of the moment, so that it will give grace to those who hear" (Ephesians 4:29).

IMAGINE A HUSBAND AND WIFE sitting at the dinner table, both silent, lost in their thoughts. Words are few, but the distance between them feels vast. A careless remark from earlier still lingers in the air. This wasn't their intention. Love is present, but so is the habit of criticism. How did they get here? Could gratitude be the bridge back to warmth and connection?

We can unwittingly build giant "Do Not Enter" signs around our hearts that hinder our relationships. Yet, gratitude holds the power to tear those barriers down. When we choose to cultivate thankfulness, our hearts become open to seeing beyond the moment; we allow God's light to shine beyond imperfections.

Gratitude is an Antidote to Criticism and Judgment

Our relationships can suffer when we constantly focus on others' flaws or mistakes. It's easy to slip into patterns of criticism without even realizing it.

When we make a habit of thanking our spouse for being kind, our friends for their support, or our children for their effort, we are choosing to look for what is right rather than what is wrong.

For example, instead of pointing out what your spouse forgot to do, you could say, "Thank you for the hard work you put in today; it helps our family." Practicing gratitude doesn't mean ignoring things, but it shifts our focus to a more positive, encouraging approach.

The world constantly tears all of us down. And as our section verse reminds us, we should be the ones to speak wholesome, edifying words that build others up.

The Power of A Simple Thank You

A simple "thank you" has the power to transform relationships. Even a small expression of appreciation can shift the entire tone of our conversations. People that share their hearts with us have trusted us. When someone shares an idea, instead of brushing it off, we can say, "Thanks for sharing with me. I can see this is important to you." In just a few words, we acknowledge their feelings and help them feel valued and heard. Over time, thankfulness softens all our conversations, encourages openness, and strengthens the bonds between us.

Gratitude Helps Us Value Others

No one enjoys being around a negative, critical person. We all know the type. Perhaps someone's face even popped into your mind just now. But it's harder to recognize how often we, too, may bring negativity into our relationships without realizing it.

Sometimes, we unintentionally discourage the dreams and aspirations of our children, spouses, friends, or co-workers. Most likely we didn't intend to discourage them. Maybe we didn't realize the careless word or offhand comment landed more heavily than we intended. Maybe words just slipped out. Maybe we didn't see the possibilities they saw, or perhaps we didn't view the person through the lens of God's love and purpose for their lives.

We often take the people closest to us for granted, speaking without thinking how our words impact their hopes and dreams. Our negative comments can demoralize them, making them feel unappreciated, unimportant, or misunderstood. But the good news is, we are on a journey to change all this!

As an illustration of this point, Sarah had always been quick to correct her children, offering "constructive criticism" at every turn. But one evening, as she overheard her son telling his younger sister, "That's a dumb idea," she felt a pang in her heart. He was simply repeating what he had heard so often. She realized at that moment that her words were breaking her children's spirits. That night, she whispered a simple prayer, "Lord, teach me to see the good in them and to speak words that give life."

Gratitude Helps With Daily Frustrations

Life is filled with an abundance of frustrations and misunderstandings: people don't do things you think they should, they act badly, they leave the empty milk jug in the frig, they drive too slowly. And then there are always endless chores. These moments can pile up, forming walls of irritation and resentment. But if we can make a habit of switching our brains to thankfulness instead of irritation, we can rewire our brains and hearts to replace impatience with gratitude and peace.

It is easy to feel overwhelmed with the chaos of daily life. For example, One afternoon, as toys covered the floor and noise filled the air, Julie felt her frustration rising. But instead of reacting, she paused. "Lord, thank You for their laughter," she prayed silently. That small shift reminded her that this season of life, chaotic as it may be, was a gift. Gratitude turned her impatience into joy.

Thankfulness Reduces Tension and Builds Trust

Gratitude is a healing balm, like the Balm of Gilead, soothing wounds of misunderstanding and softening hearts hardened by irritation and tension. In the middle of misunderstandings or disagreements, gratitude creates space for reconciliation.

For instance, imagine a heated argument brewing between two close friends. Voices rise, defenses go up, and the space between them fills with frustration. But then, one pauses and says, "I just want you to know that I really appreciate you." Instantly, the mood shifts.

Proverbs 15:1 reminds us, "A gentle answer turns away wrath, but a harsh word stirs up anger." A gentle, grateful word during conflict can change the course of the conversation and the relationship itself.

Thankfulness doesn't deny what's wrong; it simply acknowledges the goodness that exists within the other person. Even when it may be hard to see, God is always working things for good.

Joseph's example in Genesis is a powerful example. Betrayed by his brothers, sold into slavery, and imprisoned, he had every opportunity to be bitter. He could have harbored anger and resentment. Instead, he chose gratitude for God's providence.

When he finally revealed his identity to his brothers, he said, "You meant evil against me, but God meant it for good" (Genesis 50:20).

Joseph's grateful heart and trust in God allowed him to forgive and reconcile with his family. This act of grace not only restored their relationship but also ensured the survival of their family during a time of famine.

Imagine if Joseph had clung to his pain instead of choosing forgiveness. His family would have remained fractured, and his own heart would have remained heavy. The same choice lies before us—will we focus on offenses, or will we see through the lens of God's grace and forgiveness?

Gratitude blesses us with a path of reconciliation even in our most challenging relationships. By cultivating a heart of gratitude, we invite grace into our relationships. It becomes easier to resolve conflicts because we approach one another from a place of appreciation rather than accusation or resentment.

Gratitude Reflects God's Love

When we're genuinely grateful for someone, we're more likely to be fully present with them, valuing each moment we have together. Gratitude helps us slow down, listen, and treasure the time we share. In a world filled with distractions, attentiveness has become a rare gift. Thankfulness reminds us that each interaction is a meaningful opportunity to love others well.

What if a father, exhausted after a long workday, sets aside his phone to truly listen as his daughter recounts her day? What if our friend resists the urge to check emails during coffee and instead engages deeply? These moments of attentiveness communicate, "I see you. You matter to me." Being thankful enhances the quality of our relationships and reminds us to cherish each moment we have.

As we cultivate gratitude for one another, our words and actions reflect God's love and build up those around us. When we speak words that edify, we value others' perspectives, we practice patience and attentiveness, and we fulfill our call to bring, blessing, edification, grace, and healing to everyone we encounter. In this way, gratitude blesses deeper relationship connections.

Cultivating the Blessing Gratitude in Relationships

1. How often do you express gratitude to the people you see daily? What small adjustments could you make to show more appreciation in these interactions?
2. Reflect on a relationship where you may have taken someone for granted. Ask Jesus what actions or words of appreciation you can offer to make them feel valued.
3. What does it look like to see someone through "God's eyes" as mentioned in this section? How might this perspective change the way you relate to them? Jesus, what would you say to me about this?

11. Gratitude Blesses Our Physical & Emotional Health

> *"Bless the Lord, O my soul, and **forget not all His benefits**—who forgives all your iniquities, **who heals all your diseases**, who redeems your life from destruction, who crowns you with lovingkindness and tender mercies, who satisfies your mouth with good things, so that your youth is renewed like the eagle's"* (Psalm 103:2-5).
>
> *"A joyful heart is **good medicine**, but a broken spirit dries up the bones"* (Prov 17:22). *"A cheerful disposition is good for your health; **gloom and doom leave you bone-tired**"* (Prov 17:22 MSG).

LIKE A GENTLE SUMMER RAIN that falls onto hot dry ground, gratitude refreshes every part of our lives. It brings refreshing renewal and vitality to our spirits, souls, and bodies. God in His kindness is concerned about every part of us.

In our verse above, David's words remind us to not forget all of God's benefits! He forgives our iniquities, heals all our diseases, satisfies our mouths with good things, and renews our strength like the soaring eagle! He reminds us to not forget our covenant benefits with our Creator Father.

When we intentionally recount God's goodness and meditate on His amazing benefits, we practice gratitude! This act of remembrance transforms our spiritual lives and also powerfully impacts our physical and emotional health.

Science Confirms Timeless Truths

Modern scientific research confirms Scripture's wisdom that practicing gratitude profoundly benefits our health. Studies show that people who regularly practice gratitude enjoy:

- A stronger immune system
- Lower blood pressure
- Improved sleep quality
- Higher levels of positive emotions
- Increased resilience during difficult times
- Longer and healthier lives

It is remarkable to think that something as simple as gratitude can have such profound effects on our well-being. Gratitude helps reduce stress and anxiety and makes way for miracles.

Physiologically speaking, thankfulness prompts the release of chemicals in our brains that foster relaxation and happiness. This leads to better mental health, improved physical health, and overall well-being.

Heart Health and Gratitude

Scientific research shows that gratitude significantly improves heart health by reducing stress hormones and lowering blood pressure which protects against heart disease.

When we shift our focus to what we're grateful for, we help our heart function more efficiently by counteracting the harmful effects of stress. This perfectly illustrates how a joyful heart is "good medicine."

Gratitude Fosters Longevity & Quality of Life

Practicing gratitude can even lead to a longer and healthier life. People with grateful hearts tend to adopt healthier habits. They often eat better, exercise more, and avoid harmful behaviors.

Thankfulness fuels our motivation to take care of ourselves and enhances both our quality of life and longevity. Grateful people engage life with enthusiasm and embrace its amazing possibilities. Gratitude is energizing and increases our overall vitality and well-being.

Emotional Healing and Joy

Gratitude has a powerful effect on emotional health and can help reduce symptoms of depression.[35] When we focus on the good in life, it helps us shift our thoughts away from despair to focus instead on hope.

This doesn't mean that hard times disappear, but gratitude gives us a tool to redirect our thoughts and feelings from the shadows to His light. Philippians 4:8 encourages us to think about "whatever is true, whatever is honorable, whatever is right, whatever is pure, whatever is lovely, whatever is of good repute, if there is any excellence and if anything worthy of praise, dwell on these things."

Practicing gratitude is one way to keep our minds focused on these virtues to boost our mental and emotional well-being.

Choose Gratitude Over Doom And Gloom

> *"A cheerful disposition is good for your health;* **gloom and doom leave you bone-tired***" (Prov 17:22 MSG).*

Negativity, like a thief in the night, robs us of strength and obscures our vision of hope. It builds a "Do Not Enter" barrier around our hearts and blocks anyone and everyone from getting in. When we dwell on gloom, we allow discouragement to dominate our minds and we miss the evidence of God's love and provision all around us.

---

[35] This is not medical advice. If you feel like you need to see a medical professional, you do. God has graced humanity with many avenues of healing. Many times, God uses them all to bless us.

This is why we must actively choose to see life through God's lens—a perspective brimming with promise, empowering grace, and unfailing love. We must vigilantly guard our attitudes and examine the motives behind the words we speak. By doing so, we can intentionally uproot negativity and replace it with gratitude and faith-filled words.

We must choose—daily and deliberately—to remember God's goodness. Seeing as He sees opens our eyes to amazing possibilities and anchors us in His faithfulness. This inner attitude ushers us into His peace, reshaping both our physical and emotional health. Gratitude tears down the barriers of negativity and makes way for the abundant life God desires for us.

Energy and Motivation Increase

Proverbs 17:22 in The Message reminds us that negativity "leaves you bone-tired." In contrast, gratitude fuels our energy and revitalizes our spirit. It acts as a spark to ignite hope and perseverance within us.

When we're thankful, we're more likely to feel positive about what we can accomplish. It gives us the drive and inspiration to pursue our goals and tackle challenges. With a grateful outlook, we're energized to engage in life, face obstacles, and seek out growth opportunities. This focus on the positive creates an emotional lift and increases our stamina and joy.

Helps to Combat Insomnia and Promotes Restful Sleep

Gratitude has a positive effect on our ability to rest. Those who practice thankfulness often enjoy improved sleep quality. When we reflect on blessings before bed, it calms our minds, eases worry, and creates a sense of relaxation. This simple practice shifts our focus from troubles to the gifts we've received and allows our bodies to follow with peace and restoration.

By redirecting our thoughts to gratitude, we create an atmosphere conducive to peaceful and restorative sleep. Over time, this nightly habit not only enhances our rest but also bolsters physical and mental resilience, leaving us better equipped to face the day ahead. Gratitude truly acts as divine medicine for our spirit, soul, and body, drawing us closer to the abundant life He desires for us.

Cultivating The Blessing of Gratitude for Health

1. What are some aspects of your life that bring you joy and contentment? How might focusing on these daily improve your overall well-being?
2. How often do you take a moment to express thankfulness for your health, however it may look?
3. In what ways does stress show up in your life? How might regular gratitude practice help you reduce stress and find peace in those moments? Jesus, what do you say about this?

12. Gratitude Blesses us with a Powerful Weapon

"Let the high praises of God be in their mouth, and a two-edged sword in their hand." — Psalm 149:6 (NKJV)

AS WE HAVE SEEN THROUGHOUT this book, thanksgiving is much more than saying, "Thank you." It is also an inner posture of the heart that blesses us with increased revelation, grace, growing faith, success, purpose, strength, peace, contentment, God's presence, better relationships, and better health. In this section, we will look at the blessing of thanksgiving as a powerful weapon in spiritual warfare.

Whether we like it or not, a life of true peace, love, joy, contentment, and purpose requires war. There was war in the heavens when Satan rebelled, and there has been continuing war on the earth ever since. Today, we are still engaged in the same spiritual battle against forces that try to rob us of God's gift of an abundant and purposeful life.

The reason Jesus taught us to pray, "Your kingdom come, Your will be done, on earth as it is in heaven,"[36] is because God's will does not automatically happen in our fallen world. God's will is something we must pray for and actively pursue.

The enemy does not simply sit back and allow us to freely live out God's amazing purpose for our lives. He seeks to hinder us, by attacking our relationships, our health, our minds, and our peace.[37]

Yet, we don't always recognize the spiritual forces at work against us. We might attribute our struggles to "just life," or we might settle for less, thinking things can't improve.

---

[36] Matthew 6:10.
[37] Matthew 11:12.

A minister friend once told me, "You have to know when the enemy is stealing from you and shooting you in the head!" If we don't recognize how and when the enemy attacks us, we risk becoming complacent and passive. Then we let the enemy steal from us and shoot us in the head!

Whether we like it or not, this Christian life is a life of war and has been a life of war since the beginning! Because we are children of God, Satan wants to take us out! Our default position must be "fight"! We must stand up to the thief.

With Christ's authority, we can declare, "Stop! No more! We can replace the awful thoughts with thankful thoughts. Just as Jesus said, "Satan, go away," we can also say, "Satan, go away!"[38] And the Bible says, "If the thief is caught, he must pay sevenfold" (Prov 6:31). So, we can demand, "You owe me, and I'm here to reclaim what God has promised! Give back all you have stolen!"

Thanksgiving Is A Weapon In The Battlefield Of Our Minds

Our mind is the most common battlefield. When we practice gratitude, we become more aware of our thoughts AND the enemy's thoughts that come to attack us! We can catch him in the process of dropping unthankful, negative, spiteful, envious, comparison, and unwholesome thoughts into our minds. This is the tactic he uses to steal our faith, our joy, our relationships, our health, our peace, and every good thing Jesus came to give!

Because the warfare is in our minds, thanksgiving and praise are deeply intertwined with spiritual victory. They redirect our focus from our challenges to the One who is greater than our challenges. When we give thanks, we anchor ourselves in God's promises, His character, His grace, His miracles, and His unchanging faithfulness!

---

[38] Matthew 4:10.

When we thank God, we choose to trust His goodness, even if we can't yet see the end of our struggles. Hebrews 11:1 describes faith as "the assurance of things hoped for, the conviction of things not seen." Thanksgiving switches our thinking from doubt to assurance. It's a faith-filled declaration that, regardless of our circumstances, we believe and are convinced of God's ultimate power to bring us through to victory!

Remember David as he approached Goliath with only a sling and a few stones. Instead of focusing on the threat, he declared his confidence in God's might. Likewise, when we face "giants" in our lives, giving thanks to God shifts our thoughts from fear to faith. It's an act of spiritual strength and vision that sees beyond our present troubles to God's past victories—and trusts that He will come through again.

Praise With Thanksgiving Is Our Battle Song

Our verse for this section, Psalm 149:6, paints a vivid picture of praise and thanksgiving as weapons. It says, "Let the high praises of God be in their mouth, and a two-edged sword in their hand." This verse suggests that praise is not passive; it's a forceful expression of trust in God's power.

When we are struggling, praise can become our "battle song." When we lift our voices in thanksgiving and worship, we are effectively standing up in faith, declaring that God is fighting our battles.

Consider the example of King Jehoshaphat in 2 Chronicles 20. When facing a massive enemy army, Jehoshaphat put singers at the front lines, instructing them to praise God with thanksgiving. As they sang, "Give thanks to the LORD, for His steadfast love endures forever," God confused their enemy so that they turned on each other. Thanksgiving and praise led to victory in this battle.

When we, too, place praise at the forefront of our lives, it disrupts the enemy's plans and invites God's miraculous intervention.

Thanksgiving and Praise Shift Our Perspective to God's Sovereignty

In the thick of life's trials, it's easy to become overwhelmed by what we're facing. The enemy wants us to focus on our limitations, our fears, and our past mistakes. However, thanksgiving takes our eyes off ourselves and puts them on God. It shifts our perspective upward and reminds us that the God we serve is greater than any obstacle.

When Paul and Silas were imprisoned, they could have given in to despair.[39] But instead, they prayed and sang hymns of praise to God. Their voices, filled with thanksgiving and trust, led to a miraculous earthquake that broke their chains and opened prison doors. This shift from fear to worship brought freedom not only to them but to all who heard them. Thanksgiving, then, becomes a way of stepping into God's miraculous power, where nothing is impossible.

Thanksgiving and Worship Invite God's Presence into Our Circumstances

> *"You are holy, O You who are enthroned upon [inhabit] the praises of Israel" (Psalm 22:3).*

As we talked a bit about earlier, Psalm 22:3 reminds us that God lives within the praises of His people. When we worship and give thanks, we are inviting God's very presence into our lives and situations. His presence brings strength, peace, and miraculous

---

[39] Acts 16.

power. No matter how fierce the struggles may seem, God's presence turns the tide in our favor.

In times of trouble, giving thanks shifts the atmosphere. What begins as an act of faith leads to an infusion of God's presence. Can you sense His peace and presence in this moment?

When we invite Him into our circumstances with a heart of gratitude, He moves in ways we can't imagine. This becomes the doorway through which God steps into our lives to bring victory and all that we need.

As we wield thanksgiving as a weapon, we adopt a strong, victorious mindset, rooted in the certainty that God is fighting for us. And if God is for us, who can be against us?

Cultivating The Blessing of Thanksgiving in Warfare

1. Reflect on an area of your life where you feel opposition or struggle. Could this be a spiritual battle? Jesus, what would you say to me about this?
2. Reflect on the example of Jehoshaphat (2 Chronicles 20). What would it look like for you to "put praise at the forefront" of a difficult situation in your life?
3. Are there unthankful or unwholesome thoughts that the enemy has been planting in your mind? What is a specific strategy to help you remember to replace those thoughts to reclaim your faith, peace, and joy?
4. How does viewing your Christian life as the life of a warrior change your perspective on daily challenges? Jesus, what do you say to me about this?

_____
_____
_____
_____
_____
_____
_____

13. Gratitude Blesses Us With Generosity

*"You will be **enriched in every way so that you can be generous** on every occasion, and through us your generosity will **result in thanksgiving to God**" (2 Cor 9:11).*

IN OUR PREVIOUS HOUSE, we had two rows of raspberry bushes. My husband trimmed them back and tied them up every fall, and then in July we had an enormous crop of raspberries. One particular year we picked gallons and gallons of delicious red raspberries and invited friends and family to come over to pick.

One evening, after picking a bowl full of berries, our growing 12-year-old granddaughter began tossing raspberries in the air and catching (and missing) them with her mouth. We laughed as she caught (and missed) raspberries with her mouth.

I thought about the amazing moment we had giggling with the children because of the abundance of raspberries. We had eaten our fill while picking, had ice cream with raspberries piled on top, and still had plenty to spare.

If I had bought a tiny basket from the store, I would have been frantic and afraid of not having enough. We all would have eaten a couple and that would have been the end of the matter. Yet, because of God's amazing abundance, we also had amazing provisions to share with family and friends.

This is a small example of the abundance God wants to pour out into our lives. I don't know about you, but I have to remind myself occasionally that God is generous. I do not have to be stingy. God is not stingy. He wants to pour abundance into every area of our lives.

When we rely upon His grace in our spiritual growth and our physical lives, He provides a table of plenty even in the presence of our enemies. He provides refreshing, overflowing streams even in desert seasons.[40]

The Purpose of God's Blessings

In our section verse, the Apostle Paul highlights a powerful truth about God's blessings. He teaches us that God enriches us not only for our own benefit but so that we can, in turn, be a blessing to others.

In the previous verse to this one (which we studied earlier), Paul wrote about how the empowering grace of God gives us sufficiency and abundance in all things. Here, he underscores the purpose of that abundance: it is so that we can live lives of generosity that cause others to give thanks and praise to God. We can share this life of abundance with others so that our generosity brings praise and thanks to our Lord. We give thanks and praise, and then others also give thanks and praise!

So, a life of gratitude is not just for us, it naturally overflows into how we interact with those around us. When we are truly thankful for the blessings God has given, we are compelled to share those blessings with others. When our hearts are full of gratitude, we naturally seek opportunities to bless others. When we have received grace upon grace we can be gracious to others!

When we realize that everything we have—our time, talents, resources, gifts, and opportunities—are all gifts from God, it changes how we see the world. We shed limiting attitudes like scarcity, fear, lack, jealousy, comparison, and stinginess. These attitudes fade as we trust God as our Provider. We no longer need to cling tightly to the small amount we have. We tear down those "Danger: Do Not Enter" signs from our lives. We can live and give freely, knowing God's provision is endless.

---

[40] Psalms 23:5; Isaiah 43:19.

The Ripple Effect of Gratitude and Generosity

A truly grateful heart is a giving heart. When we acknowledge how much God has poured into our lives, it ignites a desire to pour out our love, kindness, compassion, prayers, talents, and resources to others. Generosity becomes a natural response, whether it's produce from our garden, our time, prayers, financial support, or simply lending a listening ear. We are not just thankful for what we've received, but we're also grateful for the opportunity to give back to others.

We can hold loosely to what we have, knowing that God's blessings are not meant to stop with us. They are meant to flow through us, to impact the lives of others, and to spread God's love to the world.

This open-hearted way of living creates a ripple effect of generosity and thanksgiving, impacting our families, communities, and beyond. The more we give, the more we reflect God's love and provision, creating a legacy of kindness and gratitude.

In this way, gratitude doesn't just transform our hearts, it transforms the lives of those all around us as well. We can spread a culture of generosity and thankfulness wherever we go. In this way, we spread Jesus!

Cultivating The Blessing of Gratitude for Generosity & Service

1. Do you see giving as a burden or a joyful opportunity? Think about how viewing generosity as an extension of gratitude can transform it into a life-giving practice. Jesus, what would you say to me about this?
2. What "Do Not Enter" signs might you need to remove from your heart when you think about God's abundance and generosity? Consider any boundaries you've placed on giving and how God might be calling you to let go of them. Jesus, shine your light into my heart and give me grace in this area.
3. In what ways has generosity from others impacted your life? Reflect on how receiving from others has shaped your own understanding of gratitude and inspired you.

_____
_____
_____
_____
_____
_____
_____
_____
_____
_____

Enjoying The 13 Blessings of Gratitude?

If this book has blessed you, would you take a moment to leave a review on Amazon? Your review helps spread the message of gratitude, faith, and spiritual growth—impacting more lives with the Good News of Jesus. Thank you for being a part of this journey!

30 Days of Gratitude Guided Journaling Exercises

Day 1:

Scripture:

"Rejoice always, pray without ceasing, give thanks in all circumstances; for this is the will of God in Christ Jesus for you." – 1 Thessalonians 5:16-18

Inspiration:

When things are not going like we want them to go, giving thanks will transform our hearts. It is the will of God to give thanks **not** because everything is perfect, but because His presence is with us through it all. We give thanks, pray, and rejoice because God's purposes are greater than our desires and struggles.

Prompt:

What is a situation you are wrestling with right now, and how can you express thanks to God in the middle of it? Jesus, what would you speak to me about this verse and my life right now?

_____
_____
_____
_____
_____
_____
_____
_____
_____
_____
_____
_____
_____
_____
_____
_____

Day 2:

Scripture:

"Therefore, as you have received Christ Jesus the Lord, so walk in Him, having been firmly rooted and now being built up in Him and established in your faith, just as you were instructed, and overflowing with gratitude."—Col 2:6-7

Inspiration:

When we are thankful for God's provision today, we can trust Him for tomorrow. Each new circumstance is an opportunity to root new faith seeds, grow them, and establish our lives in the faithful trust of a good God! When we see how God works through each circumstance, we naturally overflow with gratitude.

Prompt:

Can you look back and see areas where your faith has grown by trusting Him? What are you trusting Him for right now? Jesus, what would you speak to me concerning this verse and my life right now?

_____
_____
_____
_____
_____
_____
_____
_____
_____
_____
_____
_____
_____
_____

Day 3:

Scripture:

"Give thanks to the Lord, for He is good; His love endures forever." – Psalm 107:1

Inspiration:

God's goodness is the foundation of our lives. His enduring love surrounds us in every moment, whether we are facing joy or troubles. Life can be complex and even chaotic at times. However, when we acknowledge His constant unfailing goodness, we begin to see life through a lens of mercy, grace, abundance, and gratitude. We can trust that His love never fails us!

Prompt:

What is one specific way you've experienced God's goodness even when you may have been struggling? Can you see how his love endures? How can you give thanks to Him? Ask, "Jesus, what would you say to me today about this?"

_____
_____
_____
_____
_____
_____
_____
_____
_____
_____
_____
_____
_____
_____
_____
_____

Day 4:

Scripture:

"And let the peace of Christ rule in your hearts, to which indeed you were called in one body. And be thankful." – Colossians 3:15

Inspiration:

The AMP version explains that the word *rule* here means to act as an umpire. As we grow in awareness of our attitudes, we can allow peace to act as an umpire, deciding which feelings to allow in and which to kick out. We can follow the peace. Peace and giving thanks go hand in hand. When we let Christ's peace rule in our hearts, thanksgiving becomes a natural response. Even during uncertainty, we can follow His peace.

Prompt:

What things bring you peace? What things steal your peace? Jesus, what would you say to me today about this?

Day 5:

Scripture:

"Enter his gates with thanksgiving and his courts with praise" (Psa 100:4; 150:1).

Inspiration:

Thanksgiving opens our hearts to a deeper connection with God, and our praise magnifies His greatness. As we lift our hearts in thanks, we shift our focus from ourselves to the One who deserves all glory. Each moment of gratitude brings us closer to God, filling our lives with joy and His presence.

Prompt:

How can you begin each day by entering God's presence with thanksgiving? Take a moment to reflect on specific things you are grateful for today. Jesus, what would you speak to me about how thanksgiving affects our relationship?

Day 6:

Scripture:

"I will give thanks to the Lord with my whole heart; I will recount all of your wonderful deeds." – Psalm 9:1

Inspiration:

When we remember and recount God's wonderful deeds it takes our attention off the one thing we can't have. It reminds us of all the things we do have and strengthens our faith. As we remember all He has done, we are reminded of His faithfulness in our lives. The more we reflect on His works, the more our hearts overflow with thanksgiving. His past faithfulness gives us confidence in His future promises.

Prompt:

What are three wonderful things God has done in your life that you can thank Him for today? Jesus, help me keep your faithfulness in the forefront of my mind. What would you say to me today about this?

_____
_____
_____
_____
_____
_____
_____
_____
_____
_____
_____
_____

Day 7:

Scripture:

"Do not be anxious about anything, but in everything by prayer and supplication with thanksgiving let your requests be made known to God." – Philippians 4:6

Inspiration:

Our Lord beckons us to bring all that troubles us to Him in prayer coupled with our gratitude. The next verse says, "And the peace of God, which transcends all understanding, will guard your hearts and your minds in Christ Jesus" (Philippians 4:7). The peace of God guards your heart and mind as you learn to come to Him in faith by prayer and thanks.

Prompt:

What is one area of your life where you've been fretful or anxious? Bring that to Jesus in faith with prayer and thanks. Breathe in. Breathe out. Do you feel His peace? Jesus, what would you say to me today concerning this?

_____
_____
_____
_____
_____
_____
_____
_____
_____
_____
_____
_____
_____

Day 8:

Scripture:

"A joyful heart is good medicine, But a broken spirit dries up the bones" (Prov 17:22)

Inspiration:

A joyful heart has amazing healing power. When we cultivate joy and gratitude, it not only uplifts our spirits but also has a positive impact on our emotional and physical well-being. A joyful heart nourishes us from the inside out, while a broken or discouraged spirit can weigh us down, affecting every part of our lives. We can ask for joy like we ask for faith or salvation. Yet, gratitude is often the key to unlocking joy in day-to-day life, even when life is tough. When we make the mindset shift to focus on the blessings we have, joy naturally begins to fill our hearts and brings strength and renewal to our lives, and others around us.

Prompt:

Holy Spirit, bring to mind moments where choosing joy made a difference in your child's outlook and well-being. I ask you to impart joy to my friend today, whatever the circumstance! Jesus, what would you say about the value of cultivating joy?

_____
_____
_____
_____
_____
_____
_____
_____
_____
_____

Day 9:

Scripture:

"I will praise the name of God with a song; I will magnify Him with thanksgiving." – Psalm 69:30

Inspiration:

Giving praise magnifies God and turns our hearts toward His greatness. When we magnify Him, we lift Him higher in our minds and lives than our circumstances. It reminds us of God's amazing power and love. It is like walking outside into the warm sunshine that brightens our countenance and brings essential vitamins to our body. Praise lifts our spirits and opens our lives up to His amazing blessings to flow toward us!

Prompt:

Even if it is just a hum, offer up a song of praise to Him. How can you magnify Him for who He is? Jesus, help me to magnify you in my life. What would you say to me today about this?

_____
_____
_____
_____
_____
_____
_____
_____
_____
_____
_____
_____
_____
_____

Day 10:

Scripture:

"Bless the Lord, O my soul, and forget not all His benefits—who forgives all your iniquities, who heals all your diseases, who redeems your life from destruction, who crowns you with lovingkindness and tender mercies, who satisfies your mouth with good things, so that your youth is renewed like the eagle's"—Psalm 103:2-5.

Inspiration:

Because we are children of Abraham by faith, we are in a covenant relationship with our God. In this covenant relationship, God promises certain benefits—some of which include forgiveness, healing, redemption, and love. When we remember and stand on these promises, He blesses our bodies, souls, and spirits with peace, strength, and renewal. He heals, delivers, and provides all good things!

Prompt:

Meditate on the above verse. Jesus, what else would you say to me today?

Day 11:

Scripture:

"Through Him then let us continually offer up a sacrifice of praise to God, that is, the fruit of lips that acknowledge His name." – Hebrews 13:15

Inspiration:

Sometimes, thanksgiving feels like a sacrifice, when we are not feeling it, or when we haven't had our coffee yet. But it's in the hard moments when we push through our flesh that our praise is most powerful. In these moments praise is a sacrifice and a sweet fragrance to Him. He is pleased! When we choose thanksgiving even when it's difficult, God sees and rushes in to attend to our prayers.

Prompt:

Are you in a hard place today? Offer Him sacrificial thanks and be open to feeling His presence flowing back to you. Jesus, what would you say to me today about this verse?

Day 12:

Scripture:

"Let no unwholesome word proceed from your mouth, but only such a word as is good for edification according to the need of the moment, so that it will give grace to those who hear."—Ephesians 4:29

Inspiration:

Our words are powerful! Every word we speak can either build up or tear down those around us. God calls us to use our words wisely, to encourage and edify others in every situation. We can't impart empowering grace to others if we are filled with negativity and unthankfulness. We must eradicate even the hint of these poisonous attitudes from our lives. These seeds are from Satan himself. As we cultivate gratitude it helps us guard our tongues, because a heart full of thankfulness will naturally overflow with words that uplift and give life.

Prompt:

Think about a recent conversation—what words could you have used to build someone up? How can you use your words **today** to encourage someone else and show thankfulness in your relationships? Jesus, what would you speak specifically to me today about this?

Day 13:

Scripture:

"Whatever you do, in word or deed, do everything in the name of the Lord Jesus, giving thanks to God the Father through Him." – Colossians 3:17

Inspiration:

Every part of our lives can be an act of worship when done in gratitude to God. Every part of life can be ministry! Our work, relationships, and everyday activities can glorify God when we are thankful. Gratitude transforms even the mundane tasks of life into opportunities to honor Him.

Prompt:

What is a mundane everyday activity you can do today with a heart of thanksgiving to God? Jesus, what would you say to me today about this?

Day 14:

Scripture: "Delight yourself in the Lord; And He will give you the desires of your heart."—Psa 37:4

Inspiration:

When you delight yourself in the Lord, you shift your focus from the uncertainties of life to the certainty of His goodness. Gratitude flows naturally when you embrace His presence, trusting Him to shape the desires of your heart to align with His perfect will. Rather than striving to satisfy fleeting wants, you discover that His blessings—peace, joy, and purpose—are far greater than anything the world offers. Gratitude opens your eyes to see how He fulfills His promises, often in ways you never imagined. By delighting in Him, you cultivate a heart that treasures His gifts, both seen and unseen.

Prompt:

Ask God what it means to delight yourself in Him. Maybe write a prayer of thanksgiving, surrendering your hopes and dreams to God. Ask Him to transform your desires to align with His desires.

Day 15:

Scripture:

"Devote yourselves to prayer, being watchful and thankful." – Colossians 4:2

Inspiration:

Gratitude is an essential part of a believer's prayer life. Being watchful means staying alert to God's blessings and faithful answers, while thankfulness keeps our hearts aligned with His will. As we remain watchful and thankful in prayer, we are more likely to recognize the ways God is working in our lives.

Prompt:

What are you seeing today? What are you praying for? What can you be thankful for today? How can you remain watchful for what God is saying? Jesus, what would you say to me today about this?

_____
_____
_____
_____
_____
_____
_____
_____
_____
_____
_____
_____
_____
_____
_____

Day 16:

Scripture:

"Give thanks to the Lord, for He is good; His steadfast love endures forever." – Psalm 136:1

Inspiration:

God's goodness and steadfast love are unchanging, even when the world around us seems unstable. His love endures forever, and this eternal truth is a reason for constant gratitude. No matter who in life fails you, His faithful love never fails.

Prompt:

How have you experienced God's steadfast love recently? Take a moment to thank Him for it. Also, ask Jesus what He would say to you today about this.

Day 17:

Scripture:

"And God is able to make all grace abound to you so that always having all sufficiency in everything, you may have an abundance for every good deed." - 2 Corinthians 9:8

Inspiration:

This verse reminds us of God's limitless grace and provision. His grace is not only sufficient but abundant, ensuring that we have everything we need to fulfill His purposes. When we ask and trust in God's provision, we live from a place of confidence, knowing that He equips us with more than enough for every good work. Gratitude grows as we recognize that God's generosity flows into our lives so that we can, in turn, pour out His blessings on others. We are never lacking when our hearts are aligned with His will to do good.

Prompt:

In what areas of your life do you need to trust God's abundant grace to meet your needs? Jesus, what would you say to me today about this?

_____
_____
_____
_____
_____
_____
_____
_____
_____
_____

Day 18:

Scripture:

"I will extol the Lord at all times; His praise will always be on my lips." – Psalm 34:1

Inspiration:

When praise and thanksgiving are always on our lips, it shifts our focus from temporary troubles to God's eternal goodness. In every season of life, choosing to extol the Lord brings peace and joy. A heart full of gratitude keeps us connected to His presence, no matter the circumstances.

Prompt:

What three things are you thankful for at this very moment? Give praise for those things. Jesus, what would you say to me today about this?

Day 19:

Scripture:

"Thanks be to God for His indescribable gift!" – 2 Corinthians 9:15

Inspiration:

The greatest gift we have received is the gift of salvation through Jesus Christ. His love for us is beyond measure, and no words can fully describe the magnitude of this gift. Gratitude flows naturally when we reflect on the depth of God's love, grace, and mercy through Christ.

Prompt:

What does the gift of salvation mean to you, and how can you thank God for it today? Think about where you would be without Jesus's gift! Jesus, what would you say to me today?

Day 20:

Scripture:

"Let the word of Christ dwell in you richly, teaching and admonishing one another in all wisdom, singing psalms and hymns and spiritual songs, with thankfulness in your hearts to God." – Colossians 3:16

Inspiration:

When the word of Christ dwells in us richly, our hearts overflow with thankfulness. It becomes the foundation of how we live and encourage others. Gratitude flows from a heart that is steeped in God's Word, and it inspires us to lift our voices in worship, glorifying His name.

Prompt:

How can you let God's Word dwell in you richly today, and how will that lead to greater gratitude? What does this mean for you? Jesus, what would you say to me today about this?

Day 21:

Scripture:

"I thank my God every time I remember you." – Philippians 1:3

Inspiration:

The people God has placed in our lives are a precious gift. Paul's words remind us to thank God for the relationships we cherish. When we take time to express gratitude for our loved ones, we strengthen those bonds and reflect the love of Christ through appreciation and care.

Prompt:

Who are you thankful for today? Write down the names of people in your life and why you are grateful for them. Jesus, what would you say to me today about this?

_____
_____
_____
_____
_____
_____
_____
_____
_____
_____
_____
_____
_____
_____
_____
_____
_____
_____
_____

Day 22:

Scripture:

"The people spoke against God and Moses, 'Why have you brought us up out of Egypt to die in the wilderness? For there is no food and no water, and we loathe this miserable food.'"— Numbers 21:5

Inspiration:

As we discussed in the teaching section, the Israelites allowed their impatience and dissatisfaction to overshadow God's faithful provision in the wilderness. Even though God had rescued them from slavery and sustained them in the wilderness, they grew discontent and complained about the very food He provided. This ingratitude led to serious consequences. This incident reminds us that when we focus on what we don't have, we miss God's provision and blessings right in front of us. Gratitude, even in difficult times, helps us remain connected to God's faithfulness and the miraculous.

Prompt:

Are there areas in your life where you feel discontent or impatient? How can you shift your focus to gratitude for what God has already provided? How could thankfulness help you trust God more fully, even when things aren't perfect? Jesus, what would you say to me about this?

_____
_____
_____
_____
_____
_____
_____

Day 23:

Scripture:

"Giving thanks always and for everything to God the Father in the name of our Lord Jesus Christ." – Ephesians 5:20

Inspiration:

Thankfulness is a lifestyle, not just a momentary thought. Paul encourages us to give thanks always, in every situation and for everything. This doesn't mean everything is good, but it does mean we trust God's goodness in all circumstances. Gratitude is the posture of a heart surrendered to Him.

Prompt:

What is one area of your life where you struggle to be thankful? How can you invite God into that area today? Jesus, show me where I am not thankful. What else would you say to me today?

Day 24:

Scripture:

"Let us come before Him with thanksgiving and extol Him with music and song." – Psalm 95:2

Inspiration:

Music is a beautiful expression of thanksgiving. When we come before God with songs of praise, we join with all creation in celebrating His goodness. Singing with gratitude uplifts our spirits and opens our hearts to deeper communion with Him. Our praise is a powerful way to honor God and connect with His presence.

Prompt:

What song or form of worship helps you express gratitude to God? How can you incorporate that into your time with Him today? Jesus, what would you say to me today about this?

Day 25:

Scripture:

"I thank Christ Jesus our Lord, who has given me strength, that He considered me trustworthy, appointing me to His service." – 1 Timothy 1:12

Inspiration:

God equips us with everything we need for the calling He has placed on our lives. Paul's gratitude for being entrusted with service is a reminder that we, too, are called to serve in various ways. As we recognize that God's strength is our source, we can approach our assignments with thankfulness and humility.

Prompt:

How has God strengthened you for His service? In what ways can you thank Him for the strength He provides every day? Jesus, what would you say to me today about this?

Day 26:

Scripture:

"For I know the thoughts that I think toward you, says the Lord, thoughts of peace and not of evil, to give you a future and a hope" —Jer 29:11

Inspiration:

God has good plans for our lives filled with peace, hope, and a wonderful future. Even when we face uncertainty or challenges, we can trust that God's thoughts toward us are always for our well-being. His love is intentional, and He is always working things out for our good. When we trust in His plans, we can rest in thankfulness, knowing that His future for us is full of blessings.

Prompt:

How does knowing that God has good plans for your future bring peace to your heart? Reflect on a time when you were uncertain but later saw God's plan unfold in a way that gave you hope. How can you express gratitude for the ways He is leading you toward a hopeful future, even if it's not fully clear yet?

_____
_____
_____
_____
_____
_____
_____
_____
_____
_____
_____
_____

Day 27:

Scripture:

"You will be enriched in every way so that you can be generous on every occasion, and through us your generosity will result in thanksgiving to God"—2 Corinthians 9:11

Inspiration:

This verse highlights how God blesses us abundantly so that we can be generous to others, which in turn leads to thanksgiving to God. Generosity is a natural outflow of gratitude—when we recognize the blessings we've received, it stirs in us the desire to give. As we share what God has provided, we not only bless others but also glorify Him, as our giving becomes a reflection of His grace. Living with an open hand, ready to give, cultivates a cycle of gratitude that honors God and strengthens our faith.

Prompt:

How has God blessed and enriched your life? In what ways can you show generosity in thanks to His blessings? Jesus, I bring my life to you. What would you say to me about this today?

Day 28:

Scripture:

"The Lord is my strength and my shield; my heart trusts in Him, and He helps me. My heart leaps for joy, and with my song I praise Him." – Psalm 28:7

Inspiration:

When we trust in God as our strength and shield, our hearts are filled with joy and gratitude. His help in times of need reminds us that He is always near. Gratitude for His protection and guidance brings peace, allowing our hearts to leap for joy as we praise Him.

Prompt:

How has God been your strength and shield recently? How can you express your gratitude for His help and protection? Jesus, what would you say to me today about this?

Day 29

Scripture:

"How long shall I bear with this evil congregation who are grumbling against Me? I have heard the complaints of the sons of Israel, which they are making against Me."— Numbers 14:27:

Inspiration:

This verse shows God's deep disappointment with the Israelites' continual ingratitude and complaints despite His provision. The Israelites saw God's miracles firsthand—He delivered them from Egypt, parted the Red Sea, and provided manna, yet they often failed to trust Him or express thankfulness. Ingratitude can lead to a hardened heart and distance from God. Reflecting on their story reminds us to shift our focus from complaining to gratitude, recognizing that God's faithfulness never wavers, even when our circumstances are difficult.

Prompt:

Are there areas in your life where you've focused more on complaints than gratitude? How can you actively remember God's provision, even when things don't go as expected? Jesus, what would you say to me about this?

_____
_____
_____
_____
_____
_____
_____
_____
_____
_____

Day 30:

Scripture:

"Thanks be to God, who gives us the victory through our Lord Jesus Christ." – 1 Corinthians 15:57

Inspiration:

Through Jesus Christ, we have victory over sin, death, and every challenge we face. This victory is not something we earn; it is a gift from God. Our gratitude leads us in faith for victory. It leads us to live with confidence and hope, knowing that we are more than conquerors through Christ. Then we remember to give thanks for all the wonderful victories He has given through our relationship with Christ.

Prompt:

What victory has God given you through Jesus Christ? How can you thank Him for it today? Jesus, what would you say to me today about this?

Bonus Days:

Go back through the teaching section and journal the reflection questions by asking Jesus what He thinks. Have any of your attitudes changed? Have you noticed any change in your life? Have people around you noticed a change in you?

Appendix

How to Hear God Through Journaling

"My sheep hear My voice, and I know them, and they follow Me"
(John 10:27).

You Are A Spiritual Being & Have Spiritual Senses

In the beginning, our Creator Father formed us from the dust of the ground and breathed into us a spirit and soul. So, because you are a human spirit created in His image, you are automatically equipped with spiritual senses—just like physical senses—to hear, see, and perceive what your Creator Father is saying.

While throughout our lives we've developed our rational minds and physical senses, many of us have neglected our spiritual senses. So, exercising our spiritual senses may be a new skill for some.

However, since you are made in God's image, you **can** hear your Creator Father's voice. You've likely already experienced this in subtle ways—maybe through what is commonly called intuition or a "gut feeling." We have all sensed peace in one moment and uneasiness in others. We have passed people in public spaces that make us feel uncomfortable or "creepy." These are ways our human spirit is aware of the spiritual world around us. These are also a few of the ways we follow God's leading and prompting, even when we don't realize it! When you sense peace and love, you are sensing God's presence. When you practice the journaling exercises, you will sharpen your awareness of what God wants to communicate to you personally.

The Power of Journaling to Hear God

Journaling is a simple yet powerful tool that helps us focus and listen more intentionally to what God is trying to communicate. As you work through these exercises, you will begin to sense His voice guiding you. This is not about being perfect—it's about being open, willing, and present with God. First, we will look at how God communicates to us.

Understanding How God Communicates[41]

God speaks to us in various ways. Sometimes, He highlights specific words in the Bible that resonate deeply with us. Other times, He communicates through visions, pictures, or dreams. He may also use people, whether it's a pastor, a friend, or even a stranger. God often speaks through our personal emotions, especially through a sense of peace or unrest in our hearts. For example, have you ever felt uneasy until you did the right thing? This is one way God guides us.

Circumstances can also be a means of communication, as seen in the example of Jonah and the big fish. God can use anything He desires to get His message across to His children. Once, He even spoke through a donkey to Balaam!

However, one of the most common and personal ways God speaks is through spontaneous, flowing thoughts that come to our minds.

For the exercises in this book, we'll focus on writing down both our own personal thoughts and these spontaneous, flowing thoughts we think may come from God. As you write the thoughts

---

[41] I write about hearing God's voice in depth in my book, *How to Practice the Presence of God*.

that come to your mind, you'll soon begin to notice a difference between your thoughts and the ones that seem to come from outside yourself—those gentle, flowing thoughts that reflect God's heart.

Discerning God's Voice Versus Satan's Voice

A common way to hear God's voice is by recognizing His thoughts toward us and distinguishing them from other thoughts. We can learn to discern which thoughts come from our own soul, versus thoughts from God or thoughts from the enemy. Life is easier when we can identify the source of thoughts in our minds.

Remember the following principles to help distinguish God's thoughts from Satan's or our own.

- God's thoughts will come to mind spontaneously. God's thoughts are not our normal cognitive analytical process. When we normally think about a thing, we move from one idea to the next, then the next. When you receive God's thoughts, it will seem like an idea or thought just dropped into your mind.
- God's thoughts flow easily and are expressed in the first person. For example, Jeremiah writes, "The Lord has appeared of old to me, saying: 'Yes, I have loved you with an everlasting love; therefore, with lovingkindness, I have drawn you.'"[42]
- God's thoughts will be expressed through your own personal style and speech, just as each of the Gospel writers' personalities came through in their writings. However, His thoughts to you will never contradict His

---

[42] Jeremiah 31:3 (NKJV).

written words in the Bible. God's thoughts will always point to Scripture.
- God's thoughts will be wiser, more healing, more loving, and more concerned about your inner heart motive than your thoughts.
- Although God can shout at you, most often His thoughts are light and gentle, easily cut off by any exertion of personal self-will.
- God's thoughts will cause a special quickening reaction inside your spirit. They will cause excitement, conviction, faith, life, awe, joy, love, and peace. The thoughts of the Spirit of God will be evident by good fruit.[43] Negative or accusing thoughts are not God.
- When you embrace God's thoughts, there is grace, strength, encouragement, and joy to carry out His thoughts and words.

The following are characteristics of Satan's voice to your mind:
- Satan's thoughts and temptations appeal to your fleshly desires rather than God's principles. In other words, he presents thoughts that tempt you to fulfill a legitimate need in an ungodly way.
- Satan's thoughts barrage your mind to pressure you into action.
- Satan's thoughts highlight the things you do not have, rather than the awesome things you do have. They compare you to others and tell you that you are not good enough.
- His thoughts are negative and accusing.

---

[43] Galatians 5:22-23.

- His thoughts tempt you to doubt and fear.
- They tempt you to complain and be unthankful and bitter.
- They are stressful and confusing.
- Satan's thoughts may have a bit of truth but are twisted to imply something else entirely. His thoughts cause you to question what you know to be Biblically right.
- Satan's thoughts twist God's principles to bring doubt and distance into our relationship with our Creator and others.

As you continue to recognize the difference between God's thoughts, Satan's thoughts, and your own thoughts, you train your spiritual senses to choose the path of love, joy, and peace more often.[44]

Ask Questions to Hear God's Voice

The Holy Spirit is our Helper and is always ready to teach, guide, and direct us. Yet, as humans, we often lean on our own understanding and forget to ask for His guidance. James reminds us, "You do not have because you do not ask" (James 4:2). So, we're going to ask questions and listen carefully to recognize spontaneous thoughts that come to mind, then write them down.

In Scripture, God instructed people like Habakkuk, John, and Jeremiah to write down what they saw and heard from Him.[45] While our words are not Scripture, they can still be inspired by God and bring personal exhortation, comfort, and encouragement. Journaling in this way helps us learn to flow with the Holy Spirit and grow in the gifts He has already given every one of us.

---

[44] 2 Corinthians 10:4-5.
[45] Habakkuk 2:1-3 and Revelations 1:10-11.

As we go through the following sections, we can practice answering the reflection questions AND asking Jesus what He would say to us about each section.

Here are step-by-step instructions to listen for God's thoughts. You might want to review these steps until the process becomes thoroughly familiar.

1. Still Your Mind with Scripture

We will begin by quieting our minds and focusing on a passage of Scripture. Psalm 46:10 tells us, "Cease striving [let go, relax] and know that I am God." The King James Version says, "Be still, and know that I am God." When we still our minds and relax, it becomes easier to perceive what God is showing us. For our purposes here, we will focus on the verse I have included in each section. When we focus on the verse, we still our minds and shut out all the noise and distractions from daily life. We focus on the Word Himself!

2. Ask, Listen, & Write

Once you're focused and calm, ask God a question. Then listen for the spontaneous flow of thoughts or pictures that come to mind. Write them down as they come, without overthinking or analyzing them.

Your own thoughts tend to be analytical and follow a logical progression. But thoughts from God are spontaneous, flowing like the bubbling-up living water of the Holy Spirit within you.[46]

This journaling process is a simple yet profound way to engage in a conversation with God. **You'll record your thoughts and prayers, but also the thoughts you believe are His responses to your questions.**

---

[46] 2 Corinthians 10:4-5; Galatians 2:20; John 7:37-39.

King David did something similar in the Psalms. He would pour out his heart, and through the act of writing, his perspective often shifted from despair to hope and praise.

Don't judge the thoughts you receive right away. There will be time for that later. Just let the words flow. You'll likely find that you receive encouraging, uplifting, and comforting words—because His thoughts are higher, wiser, and more loving than our own. In this way, Jesus draws us into a deeper and more intimate relationship with Himself.

Special Note:
If you're struggling, ask the Holy Spirit if anything is hindering you. If something comes to mind, repent and give it to Jesus. This clears the way for you to hear more clearly. Then simply practice. Any new skill requires practice to achieve proficiency.

A Practice Journaling Question

1. **Still your mind.** "I have loved you with an everlasting love; Therefore, I have drawn you with lovingkindness." (Jer 31:3).
2. **Ask, Listen & Write.** "Jesus, what do you want to say to me about this verse and my embarking on a gratitude journey?"

_____
_____
_____
_____
_____
_____
_____
_____
_____
_____
_____
_____
_____
_____
_____
_____
_____
_____

Practical Ideas For Cultivating Gratitude Daily

- Memorize some verses in this book that speak to your heart.
- Start or end each day with a prayer of gratitude, focusing on specific blessings from the day and thanking God for His presence and provision.
- Each day list three things that you are grateful for, no matter how big or small they may seem.
- Add more personal times of worship to your week. Enter into His presence with thanksgiving and praise.
- Use phone reminders or sticky notes to remind yourself to pause and give thanks throughout the day.
- Volunteer or lend a helping hand with a spirit of thankfulness. Serving others is a powerful way to show gratitude and make a difference.
- Gratitude naturally leads to praise, so put on a worship song or hymn and let it inspire you to be thankful.
- Take time to reflect on significant moments in your life where you saw God's hand at work. Reflecting on past blessings helps cultivate a deeper appreciation for His continued faithfulness.
- Take a walk outdoors and observe the beauty around you. Give thanks for the creation that surrounds you.
- Practice saying "grace" before you eat. As you sit down to eat, take a moment to express gratitude for your food, the people who prepared it, and the provision that made it possible.
- Practice saying "please" and "thank you" more often.

- Take a few minutes to breathe deeply and, with each breath, thank God for something or someone in your life. This can be grounding, especially during stressful moments.
- Many people take the month of November or January and challenge themselves to practice cultivating gratitude each day in some way. One year, God had me take a whole year to intentionally practice gratitude each day.
- Write a note, send a text, or call someone who has impacted your life, even in small ways. Expressing gratitude to others strengthens relationships and reinforces a thankful heart.
- A person with a grateful heart also has the compassion to pray for others. Pray for people (without them knowing) at work, on the highway, or as you pass them in a store.
- Tell someone you are grateful they are in your life.
- Write down moments of thankfulness on slips of paper and place them in a jar. When you're feeling low or discouraged, pull out a few slips to remind yourself of God's faithfulness.
- Create a "Gratitude Jar" with your family. Each day have every member write one thing they're thankful for and place it in the jar. At the end of the week, read the notes together and thank God for His blessings.
- Show gratitude to a neighbor.
- Start a "Daily Bread Journal" to record how God provides for you each day, no matter how small.

- Use your time, talents, or resources to bless others. Generosity flows from gratitude and helps create a cycle of thankfulness and joy.
- Smile at people at work, at stores, and while you are driving, especially if you don't want to. Do it by faith.
- Send someone a gift or flowers.
- Send kind "thinking of you" texts, emails, or notes.
- List the things you are thankful for in your phone's notes app each day.
- Post something you are thankful for on social media—just be careful it doesn't sound like bragging.
- Start a "Things I am Grateful For" list and add to it as you think of things.
- Take a "gratitude break" from your devices for 30 minutes today. Write down three blessings you noticed during that time.
- Look in the mirror and thank God for your life.
- At the end of a work week, let someone know how grateful you are for them.
- Instead of saying, "I have to. . ." say, "I get to. . ."

About the Author

Cynthia K. Johnson is an ordained minister, author, and former associate pastor dedicated to equipping people with practical skills for spiritual growth and a deeper relationship with Jesus. She previously served as an associate pastor and the director of a faith-based women's rehabilitation center. Cynthia holds a Bachelor of Arts in Education/English, a Master of Divinity, and a Doctor of Ministry and Leadership.

Books

How to Practice the Presence of God: A Guidebook for Knowing God More Intimately.

The 90-Day Spiritual Awakening Journal: Simple Exercises to Discover God's Presence in Everyday Life

The 13 Blessings of Gratitude: Discover the Amazing Power of Biblical Gratitude, Book and Journal

Return to Eden, Book 1

Return to Eden, Book 2

Enjoying The 13 Blessings of Gratitude?
If this book has blessed you, would you take a moment to leave a review on Amazon? Your review helps spread the message of gratitude, faith, and spiritual growth—impacting more lives with the Good News of Jesus. Thank you for being a part of this journey!

Printed in Dunstable, United Kingdom